Exploring Vancouver

EXPLORING VANCOUVER

Ten Tours of the City and its Buildings

Harold Kalman

Photographs
by John Roaf

The Official Guidebook
of the Greater Vancouver Chapter
of the Architectural Institute
of British Columbia

UNIVERSITY OF
BRITISH COLUMBIA
PRESS

EXPLORING VANCOUVER
TEN TOURS OF THE CITY AND ITS BUILDINGS

Publication of this book has been assisted by grants from
The Leon and Thea Koerner Foundation, The
Architectural Institute of British Columbia, Greater
Vancouver Chapter, and a grant to the authors by the
Vancouver Foundation.

Cataloguing in Publication Data

Kalman, Harold D.
    Exploring Vancouver: ten tours of the city and its
buildings.

    1. Vancouver, B.C. — Historic houses, etc.
2. Architecture — Vancouver, B.C. I. Roaf, John. II. Title.

NA747.V3K34   917.11'33

International Standard Book Number 0-7748-0028-3
Library of Congress Catalog Number 73-93666

Printed in Canada by Morriss Printing Company Ltd.

To my students in Fine Arts 327/365

Contents

INTRODUCTION

This book is a history of Vancouver through its architecture. It offers a critical introduction to the social and geographical development of the city and its North Shore suburbs as seen in their buildings, the most tangible creations of their inhabitants.

The volume is intended primarily as a field guide for active participation. Its six walking tours (each about one and one-half to two hours long) and four driving tours (lengths are noted before the description of each) must be experienced to be appreciated fully. As the architecture makes up only a part of the greater physical environment that is the city, the areas between the buildings are often as interesting as the buildings themselves. The landscape, the placement of houses, the street layout, and the views are all essential parts of the urban geography. The visitor should remain alert for interesting features along the routes, which for lack of space have not been described in words or photographs.

Used instead as an armchair guide, the book becomes an illustrated historical record of the city and its buildings. The histories are, of course, presented geographically rather than chronologically; nevertheless the development of Vancouver did follow the general order of the tours.

A number of writers have quarreled over the alleged differences between architecture and building; here the two words are used interchangeably. *Architecture* has been defined since antiquity as comprising three elements: firmness, commodity (utility), and delight. Delight is described as the fruit of artistic vision that lifts architecture above *building*, the term used for structures erected by people untrained in design and having utility as their primary purpose.

The search for architecture in this exalted sense leads to the mainstream of European architecture, from classical Greece to Gothic France, Renaissance Italy, Georgian England, and thence to contemporary North America. The further one strays from this current, we are told, the weaker architecture becomes. By this measure, all North American buildings would, until very recently, have been but a weak reflection of those European; Canadian architecture would pale beside American, and Western beside Eastern Canadian.

A constructive approach to the architecture of Vancouver has no use for such a system. Our buildings should not be judged on whether they are good Toronto or bad Toronto. Vancouver has, from the start, offered the builder unique conditions — unique in terms of physical geography, social conditions, and building materials. Local buildings should be judged with respect to how well their designers have met these conditions. Some did indeed emulate the structures of Europe or the Canadian East, but always in terms of their own needs and circumstances. Others had no such end in mind, and their works should not be appraised as if they had.

Buildings were selected with several criteria in mind. Many were chosen for architectural reasons — for excellence of design; as representing a particular stage in the development of style or construction; or for visual interest, curiosity, or even ugliness. Others have been selected because they are of historical significance or because they represent a particularly interesting socio-cultural phenomenon.

This book pays little attention to architectural interiors except in the case of buildings that are open to the public. The listing of any building in this book does not imply that it is open to the public unless the public nature of the building is obvious or specifically mentioned.

This *caveat* is especially true in the case of private homes. None of the private houses shown in this book is open to the public nor should the reader trespass upon private property to get a better look at a house that may be obscured from a public road. The owners of 'invisible' houses have consented to have their homes photographed for this book; such consent does *not* extend to an invitation to intrude upon the privacy of the owner.

Information found in one place is sometimes duplicated elsewhere — or noted by cross-references — to facilitate the use of the book as a field guide. Dates not prefaced by *circa* (abbreviated *c.*) are considered accurate to within one year. When a building has been known by more than one name through the years, the least ambiguous one is given in the heading and the other(s) in the text. Private houses are identified with their original occupant, who may or may not be the present one. Where the information is available the name of the architect has been included for each building. Readers are asked to bring any errors or omissions to the author's attention.

For further aid, a glossary has been appended. A brief bibliography lists the studies that were of most help in preparing the text.

Footnotes would be out of place in a book of this kind. Their omission, however, does an injustice to those many historians, architects, and lay observers whose facts and opinions are reflected in the pages that follow. To them, and to others frustrated by the lack of sources, I apologize.

In lieu of footnotes it is my pleasure to acknowledge those persons who have been especially helpful in the preparation of this guide. My warmest thanks go to Barry Downs, who taught me much about Vancouver's new architecture, and to Edward Gibson, who opened my eyes to the perspective of urban geography and to the beauties of South Vancouver. I am likewise grateful for the assistance generously offered by Edward Mills, Deryck Holdsworth, Robert Watt, and Jonathan Petrie, as well as help received from Brahm Weisman, Nancy Oliver, Anna Maria Verster, Edmund and Garry Colchester, and Elizabeth O'Kiely. Terence Tanner and John Roberts of the Architectural Institute offered their full and generous cooperation in the planning of the book. Tanner, with help from John Spick, further assisted by designing and executing the maps. I am happily indebted to U.B.C. student research in Fine Arts 327, 365 and 565 and in Architecture 425; to these students — too numerous to acknowledge individually — I offer sincere thanks. The City of Vancouver has assisted through its helpful staffs in the Planning Department (for whom my investigation of Vancouver archictecture began as a consultant), the records vault, and the City Archives.

Gastown:
The Original Granville
Townsite

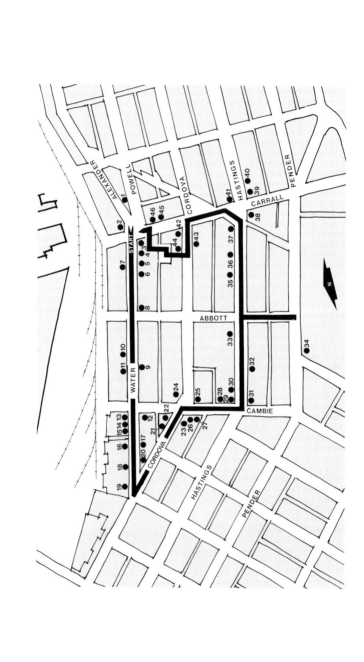

On a drizzly September day in 1867, a former river pilot named John Deighton landed on the south shore of Burrard Inlet to open a saloon for the employees of the Hastings Mill. Situated among a grove of maple trees at today's Water and Carrall Streets, the saloon of 'Gassy Jack' Deighton (his nickname was a tribute to his addiction to lengthy monologues) formed the nucleus of the settlement that came to be known as Gassy's town or Gastown.

The new townsite was surveyed by the colonial government in 1870 and officially named Granville after the British Colonial Secretary, Earl Granville. The future of the community was assured a decade and a half later when the Canadian Pacific Railway decided to extend its transcontinental line to Granville, and in April 1886 the town of Granville was incorporated as the city of Vancouver. The name, said to have been chosen by the C.P.R.'s William Van Horne, honours Captain George Vancouver, who had charted Burrard Inlet in 1792 for the Royal Navy. The 500 citizens eligible to vote in the first election chose as their mayor M. A. MacLean, a realtor; most of the early pioneers were involved either in real estate or, like MacLean's defeated rival, R. H. Alexander, in lumber.

On 13 June 1886 clearing fires west of the city were blown out of control by a sudden gale. According to contemporary accounts, the city was virtually destroyed within twenty minutes. But it recovered almost as quickly. Buildings sprang up, many of wood construction like those of pre-fire days, but many also of masonry. With the influx of immigrants between 1886 and 1892 the population grew from 5,000 to 15,000.

Vancouver's role as a shipping and distribution centre was reflected in the warehouses and wholesale stores that lined Water Street; its large transient population was served by the area's many hotels. Cordova Street became the principal commercial thoroughfare, with an electric streetcar line as early as 1890. Residential areas developed outside of Gastown, as the forests were cleared both to the east and to the west.

A severe depression struck in 1892, but ended six years later with the rush for gold in the Klondike. Many large commercial blocks and hotels were built with money acquired in the gold rush. The boom continued almost uninterrupted until the first world war. But between 1908 and 1913, when Vancouver underwent its period of greatest early growth, most of the commercial activity had moved into the Eastern Business District.

Throughout the next half century Gastown steadily declined. Ironically the lack of economic activity served a useful end; little new construction took place, but at the same time few old buildings were demolished. The area eventually contained little more than warehouses and cheap hotels for the city's poor, frequently called 'skid-roaders' after the 'skid road' on which logs were dragged to the sawmill and near which cheap rooming houses were built for loggers. The name was first used in this social sense in Seattle. The corruption 'skid row' is also often used.

Gastown began to be revitalized in the late 1960s. Old buildings found new owners and were restored as shops and restaurants. Despite Gastown's new popularity, the age of its buildings holds rent lower than in newer commercial areas.

City planners and Gastown merchants have begun to improve the streets and alleys. In February 1971 the government of British Columbia designated most of Gastown and adjacent Chinatown as historic areas, thereby preventing demolition and controlling restoration and development. Gastown's future as a lively historic quarter appears secure.

HOTEL EUROPE   **A1**
43 Powell Street
Parr and Fee, 1908-09

Angelo Colari, an Italian-Canadian hotelier who had
come to British Columbia in 1882, erected this flatiron
building as the best commercial hotel in town. It was
the earliest reinforced concrete structure in Vancouver
and the first fireproof hotel in Western Canada. The
contractors were the Ferro-Concrete Construction Company of Cincinnati, Ohio, who six years earlier had built
the first tall concrete building in the world. The Europe
with its flat brick walls and sparse decoration contrasts
with the more ornate hotels on Water Street (A3, A5,
A6). The lobby retains its original tile, marble, and brass
finishings. Architects J. E. Parr and T. A. Fee advertised
their specialization in 'the production of buildings that
will pay.... *Utilitas* is their motto, and revenue their
aim.'

I ALEXANDER STREET   **A2**
N. S. Hoffar, 1898

This warehouse originally served the ship chandlery and
hardware businesses of Thomas Dunn, a member of
Vancouver's first city council. Dunn retained the prominent architect N. S. Hoffar, whom he had chosen a
decade earlier for his retail block on Cordova Street
(A43). Hoffar successfully harmonized arched and
rectangular windows to create a handsome façade. The
fine brickwork and decorated cast-iron pillars (inscribed
with the name of Ross and Howard Iron Works) combine structural necessity with visual interest.

BYRNES BLOCK   **A3**
2 Water Street
Elmer H. Fisher, 1886-87

The cornerstone of Maple Tree Square, this commercial
block and hotel (later renamed the Herman Block) was
erected shortly after the 1886 fire by Victoria realtor
George Byrnes. The structure — one of Vancouver's first
brick buildings — stands on the site of Gassy Jack
Deighton's second saloon. Its ornate window pediments,
top-floor pilasters, and decorated cornice all publicized
the relative opulence of the Alhambra, one of the few
hotels in town then charging more than a dollar a night.
Architect Fisher was from Victoria and later made his
fortune in Seattle, where, in the first year after that city's
fire of 1889, he designed more than fifty new downtown
buildings.

THE GARAGE   **A4**
12 Water Street
McCarter and Nairne, 1930

This plain structure was an early reinforced concrete
parking garage. Today's cars outgrew their 1930-sized
stalls, and the building was transformed in 1972 by
architect H. T. D. Tanner to provide shops and offices.
Tanner created an interior courtyard surrounded by
balconies and planted with trees that opens into a series
of attractive pedestrian alleys. The site originally housed
Vancouver's first municipal buildings and — after the
fire — its first fire hall.

GRAND HOTEL   **A5**
26 Water Street
Architect unknown, c. 1890

The Grand Hotel is a fine example of the popular Victorian Italianate Style, so named because its forms adapt Italian architectural sources in an irreverent manner that is characteristically Victorian. Arches of contrasting colours and shapes cap the upper-floor windows. Particularly striking are the stilted segmental arches of the second storey. The cast-iron pillars on the ground floor bear the name of Vancouver City Foundry.

TERMINUS HOTEL   **A6**
30 Water Street
Bunning and Kelso, 1886

A curved pediment crowns the façade of this attractive structure. The upper storeys feature projecting bay windows, a common local architectural feature that probably came to Vancouver from San Francisco. Despite the individuality of its detail, the Terminus harmonizes well in scale and texture with its neighbours to the east. The name of the hotel was chosen because the city had been selected as the terminus of the C.P.R.

THIRD MALKIN WAREHOUSE   **A7**
57 Water Street
Parr and Fee, western half 1907, eastern half 1911-12

William Harold Malkin, a successful wholesale grocer
who began as a tea importer and later became mayor of
Vancouver, built three warehouses on Water Street
within eight years (see A10, A18). The simple façade of
this large Commercial Style building resembles the same
architects' Hotel Europe (A1). The lower façade (partly
a tasteful recent restoration) and roofline cornice provide
the only ornament. The impressive wood posts with their
cast-iron capitals and the timber beams and floor that
they support are clearly visible from the ground floor of
the import store that occupies the western portion.

DOMINION HOTEL   **A8**
92 Water Street
E. G. Guenther, 1900-01

The Dominion Hotel, which originally shared this building (then called the Sherdahl Block) with a ground-floor
department store, is a fine example of the Victorian
Italianate Style. Colourful arches and pilasters make its
neighbours seem dull by comparison. Brick arches inserted
into the ground floor during renovations in 1969 mar the
façade; the original rectilinear treatment remains towards
the rear along Abbott Street.

WOODWARD'S PARKING GARAGE   **A9**
130-160 Water Street
Francis Donaldson, 1971

This garage serves Woodward's Department Store (A33),
located one block to the south. The C.P.R., Woodward's,
Simpsons-Sears, and Grosvenor-Laing (now Laing)
Investments originally intended to redevelop the entire
area with a mammoth scheme called Project 200 (see
A10, A24, C12). The plan was subsequently reduced
considerably in scope and the designers came to recognize, rather than ignore, the distinctive nature of
Gastown. The fussy brickwork pattern and the arched
shopfronts of the present structure make an attempt to
harmonize with its older neighbours.

FIRST MALKIN WAREHOUSE   **A10**
139 Water Street
Architect unknown, c. 1898

W. H. Malkin (see A7) began his wholesale grocery
operation from this 5-storey structure. The top-floor
arches derive from the Victorian Italianate Style but are
less decorative here than elsewhere. In keeping with the
character of a warehouse, the rectangular windows set a
sombre mood that foreshadows the transition to the
simpler Commercial Style. The buildings on this northern
side of the block will be restored and one new building
(by Henriquez and Todd) erected as a part of the re-
planned Project 200 development (see A9).

EXPOSITION GALLERY   **A11**
151 Water Street
Arthur J. Bird, 1912

The north side of Water Street was ideally suited for
warehouses, with the waterfront and train tracks on one
side and a through street on the other. This structure is
one of the smaller warehouses in the area; most, like its
neighbours, had three or more storeys. Designer Bird later
became Vancouver's city architect. Now an art gallery —
the first of several in the area — it typifies the changing
face of Gastown.

EDWARD HOTEL   **A12**
300 Water Street
Architect unknown, 1906

On this site stood the Regina Hotel, the only building in
Gastown to survive the fire of 1886. A small group of
men trapped in the building fought to save their lives
and managed to save the building as well. In 1906 the
Regina *was* demolished — by the wrecker's hammer, not
fire — and replaced by the Edward Hotel. The simple
perpendicular lines reveal the nature of the underlying
structure. Cast-iron columns and a decorated steel beam
are exposed on the ground floor; above this the frame is
covered with rusticated stone piers and horizontal floral
bands.

MCCLARY MANUFACTURING COMPANY   **A13**
WAREHOUSE
305 Water Street
Architect unknown, c. 1899

The 300-block of Water Street contains a compatible group of warehouses, more distinguished than those on the previous block. Designers of early 'tall' buildings such as these were torn between composing façades vertically to emphasize height and trying to create a sense of classical horizontality. Here the architect has interrupted the vertical continuity of the red brick piers with white spandrels, bases, capitals, and mouldings. The warehouses in this block merit careful comparisons for their diverse solutions to this compositional problem and for the varying use of flat window heads and arches.

MARTIN AND ROBERTSON WAREHOUSE   **A14**
313 Water Street
W. T. Dalton, c. 1899

Richardsonian Romanesque is the term used to describe the style of this warehouse and its two neighbours to the west. The American architect Henry Hobson Richardson reached a compromise between history and modernity in a round-arched manner that suggested the Romanesque style of architecture without actual imitation. The mode spread west to Vancouver from Winnipeg — whence architect Dalton had come — and north from Seattle. The first local example of the style was the Empire Building of 1888 (C15). The original proportions of this wood-framed white brick building were altered by the subsequent addition of the top two storeys.

HUDSON'S BAY COMPANY WAREHOUSE   **A15**
321 Water Street
Perhaps by W. T. Dalton, c. 1897

The Hudson's Bay Company (see C4) occupied this
5-storey building, perhaps originally the tallest in Vancouver, for more than sixty years. Within the high arches
the intermediate floors appear as spandrel beams; this
'arch-and-spandrel' motif is a characteristic feature of
the Richardsonian Romanesque Style. As in the neigh-
bouring buildings, the fine brickwork is complemented by
rusticated stone trim. Twin pointed parapets top the
façade. The building was severely damaged by fire in
1972. Restoration has been delayed by the provision in
the National Building Code that restricts timber-framed
structures to three storeys.

GREENSHIELDS BUILDING   **A16**
341 Water Street
Architect unknown, 1901

Wholesale dry goods merchants Greenshields and Co. left
their name with this building despite only a few years'
occupancy following its completion. The tightly composed façade features a row of thin vertical openings
above the majestic arch-and-spandrel windows reminiscent of Richardson's influential Marshall Field Wholesale Store in Chicago (1885-87). The Greenshields
façade is enlivened by exuberant carved capitals over the
ground-floor piers depicting heads of early Vancouver's
different ethnic groups — Indian, negroid, and Spanish
types are recognizable — set in fanciful interlace back-
grounds.

342 WATER STREET **A17**
Architect unknown, 1899

The Romanesque entrance arch, with carved capitals and a grotesque keystone head, reflects the more eclectic aspect of Richardson's architecture. Above the doorway the conservative arch is abandoned and the more progressive pier-and-spandrel motif introduced (see A18). Rough-surfaced rusticated stonework provides rich texture. Rising land values motivated the addition of the two top storeys in 1911. The façade on Cordova Street curves to accommodate an alley.

SECOND MALKIN WAREHOUSE **A18**
353 Water Street
Architect unknown, 1903

W. H. Malkin (see A7) moved here from the next block (A10) to gain more warehouse space for his wholesale grocery. The 'modern' design substitutes flat window heads for arches. Vertical piers and recessed horizontal spandrels create a dynamic façade rhythm, less austere than the planar simplicity of Parr and Fee's slightly later warehouses (e.g. A7).

KELLY BUILDING   **A19**
361-367 Water Street
W. T. Whiteway, begun 1905

Wholesale grocers Robert Kelly and Frank Burnett began this warehouse complex with the erection of 5 storeys at 361 Water Street; within five years the firm — then Kelly, Douglas & Co. — had built eight more bays at No. 365 and around the corner at 367, and had sold 361 (raised to 7 storeys) to dry goods merchants Gault Bros., the present occupants. Except for steel beams in the areaway beneath the sidewalk, the structure is framed entirely in timber. Hefty 18 x 18-inch posts support the building at the basement, while each floor has narrower columns, tapering to 8 x 8-inches at the top. The pier-and-spandrel façade follows the example set by the adjacent Malkin warehouse.

HOLLAND BLOCK   **A20**
364 Water Street
Architect unknown, 1891 or 1896

The recurrent bay windows and tapered flatiron form make the Holland Block a distinctive western entrance to Gastown. The bay window was derived most immediately from the buildings of San Francisco although it found more distant ancestry in the Gothic Revival architecture of Eastern Canada and the U.S. The Queens Hotel was an early occupant of the building. B.C. Iron Works provided the block with its cast-iron piers.

HORNE BLOCK   **A21**
311 West Cordova Street
N. S. Hoffar, 1889

J. W. Horne, who made his fortune in Ontario business and Manitoba land speculation, arrived in Granville in 1885 and soon became the largest holder of real estate in the city. He served as city alderman (1888-90) and member of the provincial legislature (1890-94). As chairman of the park board he financed the beginning of the zoo in Stanley Park. Horne's office block (for a time called the Brinsmead Block) was early Vancouver's most exquisite venture into the Victorian Italianate Style. Two rows of windows are covered by decorated segmental arches and separated by grooved pilasters. The façade used to be topped by a balustrade, and a tower once rose over the Juliet balcony at the end. The Vancouver Jockey Club met here, and the Community Arts Council now occupies a ground floor office.

MASONIC TEMPLE   **A22**
301 West Cordova Street
Edward Mallandaine, Jr. (or N. S. Hoffar), 1888

Ben Springer (Moodyville manager) and Captain James Van Bramer erected this attractive building for the Masonic Grand Lodge and commercial tenants. Van Bramer had made his name as captain of the *Sea Foam*, the first steam ferry to cross Burrard Inlet (in 1868) as well as the first to sink when it exploded five years later at the Brighton wharf (see I6). The façades of the Masonic Temple and the Horne Block form a striking ensemble. As with so many early buildings, the cornice deteriorated and was removed for safety.

ARLINGTON BLOCK   **A23**
302 West Cordova Street
Architect unknown, 1887

Cordova Street, named to commemorate the Northwest's
Spanish explorers, developed into the main commercial
street of the city by 1890. The western end had many
brick buildings such as this one that opened as an office
block and became a hotel during the Klondike gold rush.
In later decades the Arlington Hotel deteriorated badly
and eventually closed. In the mid-1960s, property owners
in the area instilled new life into this building and its
neighbours by conducting a 'paint-up' campaign.

CP TELECOMMUNICATIONS BUILDING   **A24**
175 West Cordova Street
Francis Donaldson, 1968-69

The first part of the Project 200 development (see A9)
to be completed, the Canadian Pacific Telecommunications Centre was the first modern building to be erected
in Gastown. The delicacy of its vertical precast concrete
wall strips suggests the sophisticated New Formalist Style.
Red quarry tile successfully relieves the otherwise over-
whelming whiteness.

CARLTON HOTEL   **A25**
300 Cambie Street
Parr and Fee, 1899

This building represents one of Parr and Fee's earlier
attempts to develop a new commercial style. Parr had
worked in Winnipeg, Fee studied in Minneapolis; both
had been impressed by the progressive developments in
nearby Chicago. The plain brick piers (originally un-
painted) and cast-iron window units of the Carlton
depart from traditional styles. The building was erected
for a drug company and housed some professional offices,
but it became better known for the Carlton Cafe at street
level and the hotel above.

PANAMA BLOCK   **A26**
305 Cambie Street
Architect unknown, 1913

In the years before the completion of the Panama Canal
in 1914, there was much new investment in Vancouver's
future. The canal promised to make the city an important
world port serving Europe as well as the Orient. The
Panama Block was a modest celebration of the pending
event, with two brick storeys supported by cast-iron
columns. The north end reveals that the building tapers
almost to a point.

Cambie Street marks the western edge of the original
Granville townsite. The streets west of here, part of the
C.P.R.'s district lot 541 surveyed in 1885 (see p. 63),
are aligned in different directions, creating oddly shaped
lots.

313-325 CAMBIE STREET   **A27**
Architect unknown, 1889

The ground floor façade is recessed behind cast-iron
columns and reached by staircases bridging the open
areaway below street level, a common feature of English
city buildings. The upper storeys feature awkwardly
elongated brick arches spanning pairs of windows and
integrated into the brickwork.

COMMERCIAL HOTEL   **A28**
340 Cambie Street
Architect unknown, 1896

This ruggedly textured brick and stone building has
always been the Commercial Hotel; the name used to
appear on a pointed gable at the top. Ponderous ground-
floor arches are now mostly concealed by the new front.
The tiny barber shop next door, probably the smallest
building in the city, has occupied the gap between the
two large structures ever since the beginning of the
century.

*The buildings west of Cambie Street are discussed in
Tour C.*

FLACK BLOCK   **A29**
163 West Hastings Street
William Blackmore, 1899

Owner Thomas Flack 'struck it rich' in the Klondike and
spent some of his money on a building that was billed as
'the most expensive in the city of its size, a building that
Vancouverites will feel proud of.' William Blackmore,
like many other early architects, came to Vancouver
from England by way of Winnipeg, where he would have
seen buildings in this Richardsonian Style. Time has been
unkind to the Flack Block. A superb heavy, round arch
with ornate carving framed the Hastings Street entrance,
and a decorated cornice and parapet crowned the top.
Still untouched are the rusticated walls and carved capitals of the window shafts.

ORMIDALE BLOCK   **A30**
151 West Hastings Street
G. W. Grant, 1900

George W. Grant, a former Nova Scotian who practised
architecture from New Westminster, was a talented
eccentric. The Ormidale Block — also built with money
from the Klondike gold rush — inverts the traditional
Richardsonian arrangement by placing the small rectangular windows *beneath* the arch-and-spandrel row
(contrast A29). An oval window occupies the upper
right corner; a 2-storey bay window once projected below
this. The fine brickwork reinforces the quality design
which is marred, however, by the addition of a new false
front.

PROVINCE BUILDING   **A31**
198 West Hastings Street
Architect unknown (possibly A. A. Cox), 1908-09

Publisher and politician Francis Carter-Cotton built this fine steel-framed building to house the *News-Advertiser*, the first newspaper in Canada to be printed electrically. The rival *World* won admiration soon afterward when its own much taller building (A34; visible over the present building) eclipsed this structure. Both papers were absorbed into the *Sun*, published until recent years from the World Building. The building takes its present name from the *Province*, purchased from W. C. Nichol (see F2) by the Southam family in 1923. In the following year this building and its southern neighbour, the Edgett Building (by A. A. Cox, 1910), were linked by a bridge.

Builder Theodore 'Granite' Holrobin earned his nickname from a huge boulder that blocked excavation of the site. Holrobin called in blasters from Victoria to shatter the obstruction. The handsome stone arches and decorated parapet complement the relatively plain intermediate brick floors whose pier-and-spandrel treatment increases the sense of height.

RALPH BLOCK   **A32**
126 West Hastings Street
Parr and Fee, 1899

Piers of brick enclose mullions of cast iron, radical for
Vancouver although by then outdated elsewhere. The
material was probably dictated by owner William A.
Ralph, a bridge builder for the C.P.R. and Dominion
Bridge Company who specialized in iron structures. The
slightly bowed front adds a comely note. The iron per-
mitted large windows; iron mullions, although with brick
spandrels, did the same for the adjacent Henderson
Block (122 West Hastings Street), designed in 1899 by
G. W. Grant.

WOODWARD'S STORE   **A33**
101 West Hastings Street
George H. Wenyon and others, begun 1903

In 1892 Charles Woodward opened a modest retail store
(still standing) at the northeast corner of Main and
Georgia Streets. Within two generations Woodward's was
one of the largest department stores in Western Canada.
The present site began to be developed in 1903 as part of
the westward shift of Vancouver's principal retail stores.
The oldest part of the present store, a 6-storey timber
structure at Hastings and Abbott, was built in 1908. The
additions which followed — with about a dozen building
campaigns by almost as many architects — created a
cohesive architectural conglomerate.

SUN TOWER   **A34**
500 Beatty Street
W. T. Whiteway, 1911-12

Publisher Louis D. Taylor, later to become mayor of Vancouver, erected this skyscraper as a home for the Vancouver *World*. The 17-storey building — 272 feet high — succeeded the Dominion Building (C26) as the tallest in the British Empire. Its prominence was short-lived, for the Royal Bank of Canada erected a 20-storey building in Toronto in 1914. The broad base supports a slender polygonal shaft with a tall copper roof. This 'mounted tower' arrangement occurs here slightly earlier than at either the famed Woolworth Building in New York (1911-13) or the Smith Building in Seattle (1914). Financial difficulties forced the *World* out of the building in 1915. The Vancouver *Sun* was published here between 1937 and 1964 and left its name with the tower. A fine view of the area is available from the terrace of the Nine Maidens Restaurant, named for the sculpted caryatids who gracefully support the cornice half way up the building.

EASTERN BUILDING   **A35**
51 West Hastings Street
Hooper and Watkins, 1908

Thomas Hooper, an architectural conservative with large
practices in both Vancouver and Victoria, was a master
of proportion and detail. This 5-storey building rises
gracefully, despite horizontal divisions, somewhat in the
manner of Chicago buildings of a generation earlier.

33-37 WEST HASTINGS STREET   **A36**
Architect unknown, c. 1908

This curious building looks as if its workmen began from
both ends and came out unevenly at the middle. Between
the bay windows, the 'central' pilaster is flanked by three
bays on one side and only two on the other. Particular
difficulty was experienced in arranging the tiny attic
windows. The lack of sophistication reminds us that a
large proportion of local structures were the work not of
trained architects but rather of practical builders.

MERCHANTS' BANK   **A37**
1 West Hastings Street
Somervell and Putnam, 1912-13

Popular among the financial establishment, W. M.
Somervell and J. L. Putnam had offices in Vancouver
and Seattle. Their creations contrast with the plainer
buildings designed for the mercantile community by Parr
and Fee, Whiteway, and others. The Merchants' Bank is
solidly decorous in its Neoclassical garb; pilasters and
frieze in cut stone conceal a fireproofed steel frame
designed to support a future addition of 7 storeys. The
façade was angled to accommodate the C.P.R. spur line
to False Creek (see G1). The removal of the tracks in
1931 led to the creation of Pioneer Place, better known
as Pigeon Park. The park was a favourite meeting place
for skid road residents until city council removed the
benches in 1972 under pressure from local merchants.

B.C. ELECTRIC RAILWAY COMPANY   **A38**
BUILDING
425 Carrall Street
Somervell and Putnam, 1911-12

By the time the B.C. Electric built this depot, the company's interurban system was the largest in Canada,
reaching sixty miles up the Fraser Valley to Chilliwack.
Streetcars, operating since 1890, entered this building,
and the C.P.R. spur line passed by its side. When streetcars were replaced by buses and the B.C. Electric (now
B.C. Hydro) moved to Burrard Street (E1), the ground
floor was closed in for a bank. The present top storey
replaces the original steep copper roof, probably an
allusion to the railways' Château Style (see D2).

PENNSYLVANIA HOTEL   **A39**
412 Carrall Street
W. T. Whiteway, 1906

Tiers of bay windows — more than on any other Vancouver building — cover both façades of this 5-storey
hotel. The corrugated front evokes memories of San
Francisco's famed Palace Hotel (1873) which was
destroyed in that city's earthquake and fire in the year
this hotel was built. Architect Whiteway, a Newfound-
lander who worked for a time in San Diego, left his mark
in the Gastown area with his many commercial buildings.

HOLDEN BUILDING   **A40**
16 East Hastings Street
W. T. Whiteway, 1910-11

Realtor William Holden built this somewhat clumsy skyscraper to lease to Molson's Bank and other tenants. The
ground floor (refaced in 1972 in fashionable old brick)
and attic are tall in relation to the central shaft. Between
1929 and 1936 the building served as Vancouver's city
hall. City architect A. J. Bird made numerous alterations,
including the conversion of the fifth floor into a council
chamber, but no trace of the building's civic service
remains visible today.

TEMPLETON BUILDING   **A41**
1 East Hastings Street
Perhaps by C. O. Wickenden, c. 1895

William Templeton, a grocer from Belleville, Ontario, who became Vancouver's sixth mayor, built the first brick building in Vancouver on this site in the summer of 1886. The present structure is a replacement of the following decade. Brickwork with rugged stone trim creates a richly textured façade. Pilasters dress up the Carrall Street front but not that on Hastings, showing that the former was the more important thoroughfare in the 1890s. Templeton's Ontario Grocery shared the block with a harness shop and a liquor store.

BOULDER HOTEL   **A42**
1 West Cordova Street
R. MacKay Fripp, 1890

The Boulder Hotel is one of the few surviving buildings in Vancouver designed by R. MacKay Fripp, one of the leading architects of his time. Born and trained in England, Fripp reached Vancouver in 1888 via Australia and New Zealand. In contrast to the Victorian complexity of many of Fripp's works, the Boulder is sublimely simple; indeed it was one of the two earliest buildings in Vancouver to have plain rectangular windows set into an unornamented masonry wall. (The other was the Oppenheimer brothers' store; see B30.) The rusticated stonework offers compensatory texture. The third storey, added about a decade later, blends successfully with the original structure.

LONSDALE BLOCK A43
8-28 West Cordova Street
N. S. Hoffar, 1889

This broad building was erected as the Dunn-Miller Block by two of Vancouver's leading businessmen: Thomas Dunn, a merchant and alderman, and Jonathan Miller, a merchant, teamster, and first constable and postmaster. The tenants above Dunn's hardware store included the Knights of Pythias, the Vancouver Reading Room, the city's first synagogue, and the Vancouver Electric Railway and Light Company (later absorbed into the B.C. Electric Railway Company). A. H. Lonsdale purchased the building during the Klondike era. The unified façade recalls the 'terraced' buildings of Georgian England. Twin pediments at the top and the smaller pedimented window heads impart a classical flavour. In 1973 the Army & Navy Department Store began to restore the façades of this building and its two western neighbours (built 1890-92) and to rebuild the rear portions (by Paine and Associates).

STANLEY HOTEL A44
21 West Cordova Street
Architect unknown, c. 1907

This building pleases by its proportions rather than by ornament. The Stanley and its neighbour, the New Fountain Hotel, were renovated in 1971 by Henriquez and Todd in an innovative project assisted by CMHC that combined commercial activity with rent-controlled, low-cost housing. A passageway was cut through the hotel, opening onto Blood Alley Square, which in turn leads to Gaoler's Mews and to Water and Carrall Streets.

KING'S HOTEL   **A45**
208 Carrall Street
Architect unknown, c. 1888

Small yet tastefully pretentious, the King's Hotel (formerly the Tremont Hotel) has the window pediments and bracketed cornice of the Italian Renaissance Revival Style. A balcony originally protruded from the second floor, as in many of the post-fire wooden hotels. The treatment contrasts with the arches of the adjacent building at 214 Carrall Street (1889) and the austere planar façade of Parr and Fee's Filion Block at 204 Carrall Street (1909). Despite their stylistic differences, the three buildings and their northern neighbour (A46) display remarkable homogeneity in size, scale, and composition.

SECOND FERGUSON BLOCK   **A46**
200 Carrall Street
Architect unknown, begun 1886

Stilted arched windows with incised lines and keystones are imaginatively grouped into pairs on the Powell Street front, and a bracketed cornice caps the façade. This building and its pre-fire predecessor, both erected by railway tunnel-builder A. G. Ferguson, contained the C.P.R. land offices.

Walking Tour   B

Chinatown
and Strathcona

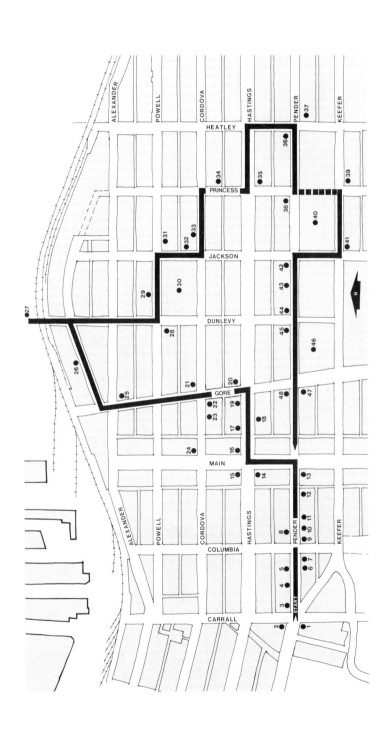

CHINATOWN AND STRATHCONA

British Columbia's large Chinese population began to arrive during the Cariboo gold rush of 1858. Two decades later more Asians were brought in by C.P.R. contractors to work on the railway. With the completion of the tracks, Vancouver's Chinese settled around Dupont Street (now East Pender), then on marshy land along the shore of False Creek. Their concentration into a distinct China-town was motivated in part by the need for protection. The non-Asian population regarded the Chinese as a competitive threat on the labour market, and in 1887 and 1907 the city was rocked by anti-Oriental demonstrations.

Despite such discriminatory actions as a federal head tax on Asian immigrants and a total prohibition on Chinese immigration between 1923 and 1947, Vancouver's Chinese community steadily grew in size and prosperity. The lively commercial centre on East Pender Street has a distinctly Chinese style of architecture with recessed balconies and picturesque rooflines. Characteristic of the architecture of China, the balconies are uncommon elsewhere in North America; San Francisco's renowned Chinatown, for example, displays ornate balconies that extend over the sidewalk. The western edge of Chinatown, around Carrall Street, catered to the entertainment needs of all levels of Vancouver society with its Opera House, red light district, and opium factories. The Asian residential area was located east of Main Street (originally called Westminster Avenue).

The East End of the city developed after the Hastings Mill was opened in 1865 by Captain Edward Stamp. Like Hastings Townsite further east (see I6), the sawmill was named after Admiral G. F. Hastings of the British naval squadron at Esquimalt. The mill company's store (H11), post office, and school made the settlement an important community even after the development of the Granville townsite.

In the following two decades, the East End developed around the mill as the domain of the political and industrial elite of pre-railway Vancouver — men like mill manager R. H. Alexander (see B25; a defeated candidate for first mayor of Vancouver), Dr. Israel W. Powell, and brothers David and Isaac Oppenheimer (B30), men whose names have been commemorated in the district's streets and parks. The development of this area east of Main Street saw wealthy industrialists crowded in by blue-collar workers, whites by immigrant Chinese and

Japanese. The physical development was consequently haphazard. Residential, commercial, and industrial buildings have co-existed happily, creating visual confusion but allowing a healthy social and economic mixture of uses.

The railway brought great prosperity to Vancouver. Many of the new arrivals, mostly Eastern Canadians, had their own — and often divergent — ideas about the course that Vancouver should take. They were regarded ambivalently by the established elite as a stimulus to the economy but also as a threat to the prevailing social order. Those associated with the C.P.R. began to settle in the West End and to develop a commercial and social centre distinct from the East End. By the time of the first world war the financial and political strength of the East End had all but dissolved, and most of the wealthy residents had moved to the West End or Shaughnessy Heights.

The physical decline of the East End, known today as Strathcona (ironically after Lord Strathcona of the C.P.R.), was steady. Little new construction occurred after 1914. Many houses were inadequately maintained. Low rents attracted poorer European and Asian immigrants who nevertheless developed a strong sense of community.

In 1950 the first of a number of schemes was proposed for urban renewal of Strathcona. A 20-block area designated as 'blighted' was to be bulldozed and rebuilt, with entire neighbourhoods and more than 7,000 people, largely Chinese Canadians, dislocated. Reconstruction began in 1962 with the first stage of the McLean Park Housing Project (B46).

Opposition to total redevelopment mounted, especially after the city's resolution in 1967 to build a freeway through Chinatown; outraged citizens forced city council to reverse its decision and the freeway was stopped. Success led to the formation of the Strathcona Property Owners and Tenants Association (SPOTA) to oppose urban renewal. In 1969 city council approved a plan for rehabilitation rather than redevelopment. In 1971 the federal and provincial governments offered to co-operate with the city in a $5 million experimental project to provide funds for the repair of older buildings. Under the terms of the Strathcona Rehabilitation Project, grant/loans are available from the combined three levels of government. The loans are up to $3,000 per house of which 75% is an outright grant and 25% is repayable without interest within five years. The city is also improving the badly deteriorated services. By the autumn of 1973, more than 270 of the 500-odd eligible home-owners had applied for grants, and 125 projects had been completed.

The following tour of Chinatown and Strathcona should be planned to leave time for lunch or dinner in one of the many Chinese restaurants in the area. Most of the restaurants are located on East Pender Street in the first block on either side of Main Street. Chinese fruit and vegetable shops are concentrated in the area around Pender and Gore Streets.

SAM KEE BUILDING   **B1**
8 West Pender Street
Architect unknown, 1913

According to Ripley the narrowest building in the world, this 4-foot 11-inch-deep structure was built out of spite by prominent businessman Sam Kee. The city had expropriated most of Kee's property to widen Pender Street but refused to compensate him for this narrow remaining strip; his neighbour, in turn, expected to receive the strategic corner property very cheaply. Kee responded by erecting the narrow building, using bay windows to advantage for extra space. The basement with its now unused communal baths extends well under the sidewalk. Shanghai Alley, to the west of the building, was once an important street in Chinatown; its remaining residential buildings have façades on both the alley and on Carrall Street.

CHINESE FREEMASONS BUILDING   **B2**
1 West Pender Street
Architect unknown, c. 1901

The architectural styles of Vancouver's two principal racial communities are married in this handsome building, just as the Chinese Freemasons combined the traditional Chinese tong or fraternal association with European Freemasonry. The building presents a Victorian Italianate façade towards Caucasian Carrall Street, while the Pender Street front, facing the original Chinatown, is distinctly Asian in character. Recessed balconies, the most typical feature of Vancouver's Chinese architecture, dominate the two upper storeys. Chinese revolutionary leader Sun Yat-sen is reported to have lived here during a residence in Canada.

CHINESE TIMES BUILDING   **B3**
1 East Pender Street
W. T. Whiteway, 1902

Local businessman Wing Sang (see B5) built this bay-windowed structure. The largest of Vancouver's several Chinese newspapers has been published here since 1939. The printing press, which uses 5,000 different characters, is visible through the window. As in most of the buildings on the block, a 'cheater storey' (so named because its area was not assessed for taxes) is inserted between the first and second floors.

YUE SHAN SOCIETY BUILDING   **B4**
37 East Pender Street
W. H. Chow, 1920

W. H. Chow, one of the few Chinese architects to practise in Vancouver in earlier years, designed a number of structures along East Pender Street. Most of his buildings have either been demolished or have suffered from later alterations (e.g. 141 East Pender Street, 1921).

WING SANG BUILDING   **B5**
51-69 East Pender Street
Architect unknown, 1889; T. E. Julian, 1901

The petite Victorian Italianate portion at the left, inscribed 1889, is one of the oldest buildings on the street and pre-dates the development of a recognizable Chinese architectural style. The larger building with bay windows was constructed around it a decade later. The building was owned by wealthy contractor Wing Sang, as was the large tenement block behind that opens into Market Alley and once contained an opium factory. Opium manufacture for export was legal; only domestic consumption was against the law. Numerous opium factories on Market Alley and Dupont Street (now East Pender Street) gave the air a strong, pungent aroma. Wing Sang also built the large but homely Woods (now West) Hotel nearby at 444 Carrall Street (by J. G. Price, 1912).

80 EAST PENDER STREET   **B6**
Architect unknown, c. 1900

A pair of bay windows with brick arches and gables give this modest building considerable charm.

88 EAST PENDER STREET   **B7**
Architect unknown, 1904

This rather plain building once served as the terminus of the Vancouver, Westminster and Yukon Railway, which first linked Vancouver with Seattle in 1904. On the western wall there is still a sign reading 'V.W. & Y.R. — To Trains' and pointing to the platform formerly located behind the building. The Great Northern Railway, which financed and later absorbed the V.W. & Y., filled in a portion of False Creek along the south side of this block and laid its tracks upon the fill. The space was found to be too restricted for the site of its transcontinental terminal, so the Great Northern acquired terminal rights at the eastern end of False Creek (see G22). Now devoted mainly to parking, the former trackland west of this building has been suggested as the site of a Chinese cultural and community centre.

CHINESE SCHOOL   **B8**
123 East Pender Street
J. A. Radford, 1921; G. L. Southall, associated architect

Recessed balconies on the second and third storeys are embellished by an ornamented parapet with the date, Chinese inscription, and four projecting finials. Intricate woodwork frames the windows of the mezzanine cheater storey. A long wooden staircase leads up to the Mon Keang School sponsored by the Wong Kung Har Tong Society. Chinese children attend the school after their regular day in the Vancouver public school system. It was the first in Canada to offer classes at the high-school level in Chinese.

CHINESE BENEVOLENT ASSOCIATION   **B9**
BUILDING
108 East Pender Street
Architect unknown, 1909

The Chinese Benevolent Association, a strong community group formed in 1908 in response to racial discrimination and now a general interest organization, erected the earliest example of the characteristic Chinatown style. The façade is recessed at every storey behind the building line which is defined by the wrought-iron balconies and the rusticated stone wall at either side.

116 EAST PENDER STREET   **B10**
C. K. L. Sihoe, 1960

Several recent Chinatown buildings have adopted the traditional recessed balcony motif. Here the arched balconies contrast with flat strip windows and stucco spandrels. The Chinese Freemasons (relocated from B2) and the B.C. Buddhist Temple occupy the upper storeys.

CHIN WING CHUM SOCIETY BUILDING **B11**
160 East Pender Street
R. A. McKenzie, 1925

A number of buildings on East Pender Street were erected
by Chinese voluntary associations which occupy the
upper storeys and lease the ground-floor shops. This particularly fine example of a tall balconied building with
a broken skyline was designed for a clan association by an
architect who had practised for more than five years in
North China. A pediment supported by Tuscan columns
reveals the inescapable influence of western architectural
tradition.

BANK OF MONTREAL **B12**
178 East Pender Street
Birmingham and Wood, 1971

A local firm of architects designed this flamboyant essay in
'Chinese Modern.' Concrete block walls create the façade
recesses and broken roofline associated with the older
architecture. Ornamental dragons decorate the top. The
successful attempt to integrate this building into its
particular environment contrasts with the hard-edged
International Style of the Bank of Montreal's former
branch at 138 East Pender (by Gardiner and Thornton,
1949).

CANADIAN BANK OF COMMERCE   **B13**
501 Main Street
V. D. Horsburgh, 1915

Bossed terra cotta columns which dwarf the passerby combine the classical sources and largeness of scale characteristic of the Edwardian Baroque Style. The *maestoso* effect fortunately distracts from the lesser detail which, upon close inspection, is disappointingly shallow.

CARNEGIE LIBRARY   **B14**
S.W. Corner Main and Hastings Streets
G. W. Grant, 1902-03

Steel magnate and philanthropist Andrew Carnegie donated $50,000 to build Vancouver's representative of the many Carnegie Libraries around the English-speaking world. The site was formerly a market and next to an early city hall (see G12). It was selected by plebiscite after West End residents had waged an unsuccessful battle to have the library erected in their part of the city. Architect Grant provided an appropriately monumental design; domed Ionic portico, Romanesque rustication and windows, and French mansard roof co-exist in surprisingly attractive harmony. The spiral iron, steel, and marble interior staircase allows a view of the fine stained glass window. The building will soon be renovated by Architects Downs/Archambault to house city health and welfare offices. The library was relocated to Burrard Street in 1957 (D37).

FORD BUILDING   **B15**
193 East Hastings Street
B. Davidson and Son, 1911

Two checks in the façade allow natural light — however
little — to reach the inside offices of this large building;
the resulting tripartite composition offers a stately expression of the Commercial Style. The building was originally
called the Dawson Building.

BANK OF MONTREAL   **B16**
390 Main Street
Honeyman and Curtis, 1929-30

This branch bank demonstrates the survival of the Neoclassical manner for banks long after the style was considered old-fashioned. As suggested below (see C6), the
Bank of Montreal may have deliberately perpetuated the
style.

235 - 257 EAST HASTINGS STREET **B17**
Various architects, 1901-1913

Seven different buildings occupy this block. Each on its own 25-foot-wide lot, they range from 1 to 8 storeys in height. Despite their manifest differences, a remarkable homogeneity persists. They share such features as bay windows and crowning cornices (or the decorative cresting of No. 239, a charming building). Architects and dates for each are: No. 235 (Empress Hotel), F. N. Bender, 1912-13; No. 237, H. B. Watson, 1908; No. 239, Blackmore and Son, 1904; No. 245, architect unknown, 1903; No. 249, A. J. Bird, 1912; No. 253, W. H. Preston, 1903; No. 257, T. U. Barber, c. 1901.

SHAW THEATRE **B18**
254 East Hastings Street
Philip W. Harrison, 1971

This handsome cinema respects the size and scale of its older neighbours. Its design may be appreciated by comparing its height, window levels, and whiteness to the F. Morgan Building (see F12) immediately to the right (by W. C. Stevens, 1910). The structure is a good example of the Brutalist Style, its deep entrance reveal and the marks of the wooden forms emphasizing the massiveness of concrete. The theatre shows Chinese films (with English subtitles) produced in Hong Kong by Shaw Brothers.

ORANGE HALL   **B19**
341 Gore Street
J. Gillott, 1904-07

The Grand Orange Lodge of B.C. erected this stalwart building as its fraternal hall. After a later stint as a wrestling arena, the structure was converted by the National Housing Administration into wartime residential suites with the insertion of two intermediate storeys (by W. F. Gardiner, 1944). The design reveals the persistence of the Richardsonian Romanesque in the attractive stone entrance arch with its carved capitals and low piers.

SALVATION ARMY TEMPLE   **B20**
301 East Hastings Street
Mercer and Mercer, 1949

The style of the regional headquarters of the Salvation Army might be termed 'Late Modernistic Neoclassicism.' The temple idea is conveyed by the assertive horizontal and vertical lines and the overall whiteness. Modernistic ornament appears in the bevelled corners and notched 'buttresses,' here achieved in poured concrete. The best indicator of early modernism is the lettering on top.

The visual sloppiness of this neighbourhood, occasioned by its unplanned development, can be appreciated by looking eastward along Hastings Street. Houses, small commercial buildings, and large hotels stand side by side along the thoroughfare.

ST. JAMES ANGLICAN CHURCH   **B21**
N.E. Corner Cordova and Gore Streets
Adrian Gilbert Scott, 1935-37; Sharp and Thompson, associated architects

Powerful massing carries the composition of this monumental church upward from the low-angled entrance to the cross on the steep octagonal roof. Pointed lancet windows, a reticulated parapet, and stylized gargoyles are inspired by the Gothic Revival, while the interior, with its round arches, has distinctly Byzantine overtones. (Designer Scott, a member of England's architecturally celebrated Scott family, had just completed a cathedral in Cairo.) The traditional modes are brought up to date by the broad surfaces, hard edges, and angular ornament of the Modernistic Style. The church is built of exposed reinforced concrete (regrettably painted in 1972), with an 8-inch outer wall and 5-inch inner wall separated by a 2-foot air space that imparts depth to the window and arch reveals. The constricted site between the clergy house (by Sharp and Thompson, 1927) on Cordova Street and the large parish hall (1925) on Gore Street inspired an ingenious cruciform plan with a Lady Chapel to the east. St. Luke's home for the poor and aged (by Sharp and Thompson, 1924) stands just east on Cordova Street.

FIRE HALL NO. 2   **B22**
270 East Cordova Street
W. T. Whiteway, 1905

This large fire station was originally the headquarters of
the Vancouver Fire Department. Renaissance arches with
decorated terra cotta capitals support a cornice once
crowned by a pediment. The formality of this design
contrasts with the domestic manner of smaller stations in
residential neighbourhoods (I5). Vancouver had one of
the earliest motorized fire departments in North America.
A 'self-propelled' engine — the first in Canada — joined
the force in 1908, and the last horse was retired in 1917.
Fire Hall No. 6 at 1500 Nelson Street (1912; passed
while returning from the end of Tour E) was reportedly
the first on the continent to be designed for trucks.

CORONER'S COURT   **B23**
240 East Cordova Street
A. J. Bird, 1932

The Georgian Revival — popular in the 1930s in Eastern
Canada but not in the West — appears in all its charm
in this building with its tidy brick, pedimented door and
artificial stone trim.

PROVINCIAL COURT BUILDING   **B24**
222 Main Street
Harrison/Plavsic/Kiss, associated architects, 1972-74

Imposing piers and walls of sandblasted concrete trans-
late the traditional columned court house façade of cut
stone (see D1) into a contemporary vocabulary without
any sacrifice in dignity. The numerous police and magis-
trates' courts scattered around the area will soon be
centralized in this new facility. Largest among the older
buildings is the Public Safety Building (1950) at 312
Main Street.

VANCOUVER AND VICTORIA STEVEDORING   **B25**
COMPANY LIMITED
300 Alexander Street
Architect unknown, 1922

This stucco commercial building in the Spanish Colonial
Revival Style is set in a now undistinguished neighbourhood that once contained the finest homes in the East
End. Hastings Mill manager R. H. Alexander lived on
this site, and other well-to-do early British Columbians
had houses nearby. No trace remains of the former good
life. The anchor on the central shaped parapet is a
reminder of the building's original maritime use; a sharp
eye still can pick out remnants of the faded inscriptions
'V.V.S. Co. Ltd.' and 'A.D. 1922.'

WAREHOUSES
300-Block Railway Street

B26

No. 329: Babcock Fisheries Ltd. (originally Martin, Robertson, and John Burns)
Architect unknown, 1910

No. 339: Paramount Salvage Co. Ltd. (originally Imperial Rice Milling Co.)
Honeyman and Curtis, 1911

No. 343: Traders Service Ltd. (originally temporary police court)
Architect unknown, 1913

No. 349: Fred C. Myers Ltd. (originally G. H. Cottrell)
Baynes and Horie, 1920

No. 365: J. Phillips and Co. (originally Fleck Bros.)
Architect unknown, 1949

No. 395: Empire Stevedoring Co. Ltd.
Watson and Blackadder, 1941

The 300-block of Railway Street has some of the finest classic warehouses in Vancouver. Nos. 329 and 339 show the two principal variants of the Commercial Style, the former with flat walls and the latter with vertical articulation. No. 349 reverts to the flat wall with segmental headed windows. No. 365 is more modern with its narrow windows and horizontal bands, somewhat in the manner of contemporary West End apartments (E12). No. 395 is a fine example of the Modernistic manner, with fluted 'pilasters' in shallow relief (achieved by fixing corrugated iron to the inside of the concrete framework) and characteristic lettering at the top. Behind their brick and concrete fronts the buildings are primarily of heavy timber construction. For newer warehouses, one should look at the industrial developments near the tracks along the eastern end of False Creek (see G21) and eastward on Grandview Highway or by the Fraser River on Marine Drive (H25).

HASTINGS MILL OFFICES   **B27**
Foot of Dunlevy Street
B.C. Mills, Timber and Trading Company, c. 1906

This charming building unexpectedly set in a landscaped patch beside a marine container dock facility was the headquarters of the National Harbours Board for many years until 1973 when it became a seamen's mission and club. The structure originally served as the offices of the Hastings Mill (p. 33), which ceased operation here in 1929 to make room for port expansion. The cheery blue and white building, with a broad verandah and large dormer windows in its hipped roof, may be identified as a prefabricated frame structure by the 4-inch vertical posts that divide the walls of narrow clapboard into 3-foot units. It was produced by the B.C. Mills, Timber and Trading Company, a giant (for its time) lumber conglomerate controlled by John Hendry (see F25) that had acquired the four largest sawmills in the province, including the Hastings and Moodyville Mills. Three granite monoliths by sculptor Gerhard Class (1965-66) were erected beyond the building to commemorate the centenary of the Hastings Mill. While walking from here to the next building, notice the original wood paving blocks that appear beneath the worn asphalt on Dunlevy Street and on other East End roadways. The roads began to be repaved in 1973.

NEW WORLD HOTEL **B28**
396 Powell Street
Townsend and Townsend, 1912-13

Banker and importer S. Tamura built this brick block
with its columns and heavy bracketed cornice to accommodate the New World Hotel and a number of Japanese
commercial and residential tenants. This part of Powell
Street is the centre of Vancouver's Japantown; import
stores and restaurants lie beyond the hotel. Japanese
immigrants arrived in large numbers early in the century.
Their population was estimated at 15,000 in 1913. In
1942, after the outbreak of the Pacific phase of the second
world war, coastal Japanese Canadians were removed to
the Interior and Japantown lay dormant, but life has
now returned to the area.

433 POWELL STREET **B29**
Architect unknown, c. 1890

'Boomtown' buildings such as this and its neighbours at
Nos. 423, 429, and 451 Powell Street — the kind most
often seen in Western movies — were common in Vancouver immediately after the 1886 fire. An easy-to-build
gabled roof is concealed by a flat-topped false front that
imitates the straight parapet of masonry construction.
The original occupants of this block were English, but
shortly after the turn of the century virtually all the
inhabitants were Japanese.

OPPENHEIMER PARK   **B30**
Powell Street between Dunlevy and Jackson Streets
Dedicated 1902

The park honours David Oppenheimer, who served as Vancouver's second mayor from 1888 to 1891. Oppenheimer was one of five brothers who arrived in British Columbia in 1856 and became the leading businessmen of Yale during the Cariboo gold rush. David and Isaac Oppenheimer both settled in Vancouver and became involved in business, real estate, and politics. Their wholesale grocery store at 100 Powell Street (by N. S. Hoffar, c. 1889) survives as an import shop. A metal bust of David Oppenheimer can be seen in Stanley Park across from the park board offices (see E26). One of Vancouver's first two public playing fields, the park was originally called the Powell Street Grounds. In the depression it was frequently the site of labour rallies. Behind the park stands Oppenheimer Lodge (430 East Cordova Street, by Erickson/Massey, 1973), a public housing project for single men financed by the three levels of government.

VANCOUVER BUDDHIST CHURCH   **B31**
220 Jackson Street
Architect unknown, c. 1906

This shingled church with the traditional gable and corner tower was taken over by Welfare Industries when the Japanese population was dispersed in the forties. It has since been returned to its original use. The hanging arch in the centre is a feature found in many houses of the period.

230-248 JACKSON STREET   **B32**
Architect unknown, 1906

These four clapboard houses bring us into the residential district of Strathcona. With a front porch, a bay window beside the door, and a gabled attic above the second floor, they are typical of houses erected between about 1900 and 1910 in both the East and West End (see B39, B43, and E8).

MARGARET MCKELVIE HOUSE   **B33**
513 East Cordova Street
Architect unknown, c. 1903

The 500- and 600-blocks of East Cordova Street contain some fine early houses (mostly built c. 1890-1905) displaying a love for wood. The illustrated house is sparkling white with bright green and red trim. The woodwork is ornate; the balcony posts and railing are turned with the lathe, whereas the flat gingerbread at the top of the balcony and within the gable is cut with the scroll saw. The walls are covered in shiplap siding, a technique soon to be superseded by bevelled clapboard (see B32). The presence of a poultry plant in the block indicates the mixture of activities common in the East End.

390-396 PRINCESS STREET **B34**
Architect unknown, perhaps c. 1900

This pair of small cabins serves to remind the visitor that Strathcona was, from the start, an area of contrasts. The poor and the rich lived side by side; homes and industries co-existed. Cottages such as these were usually rented to recently arrived immigrants.

612 EAST HASTINGS STREET **B35**
E. E. Blackmore, 1910

This retail shop built for George Simons conceals a crowded 3-storey tenement block entered from a narrow alley along the eastern edge of the property. The shiplap houses on Princess Street are a part of the same residential complex.

425-447 HEATLEY AVENUE

B36

Architect unknown, 1903

These six identical small houses have one full storey and an attic floor within the slope of the roof. Two front porches have been filled in for extra space and the walls of four units, originally clapboard, covered with composition shingle. The larger turreted house across the street at No. 450 was built by undertaker Thomas Edwards (1905).

GIBBS BOYS' CLUB

B37

700 East Pender Street

Architect unknown, 1917

Schara Tzedeck Congregation erected this building in 1917 as the first permanent synagogue in Vancouver. The round-arched doors and windows, the wall buttresses, and the Spanish tile rooflets were evidently intended as Romanesque Revival with Mediterranean flavour, a popular idiom for Canadian synagogue architecture. When the synagogue was moved to Oak Street in 1948, local sportsman Rufus Gibbs bought the building, converted the sanctuary into a gymnasium, and donated it to the Vancouver Boys' Club Association.

ST. FRANCIS XAVIER CHURCH
579 East Pender Street
J. G. Price, 1910

B38

The changing occupants of this church reflect the many nationalities who have lived in Strathcona. This imposing brick-faced church now administering to the Chinese-Canadian Catholic community formerly served as the First Swedish Evangelical Lutheran Church, St. Stephen's Greek Catholic Church, and St. Mary's Ukranian Greek Catholic Church.

602-630 KEEFER STREET
Various architects, 1902-06

B39

This group of five houses represents the two principal kinds of dwelling popular in Vancouver around the turn of the century. Nos. 602 and 620 (the latter probably by J. E. Vickers) display the pointed gables with decorative bargeboard (popularly called gingerbread) that derive from the mid-nineteenth-century Gothic Revival cottages of the eastern U.S.A. and Canada. The bay windows and the corner turret of No. 602 (built for the principal of Strathcona School) point to the same source. Nos. 612, 626, and 630 (probably by W. Cline) are more cubical with hipped roofs, British in cultural inspiration and Italianate in original formal source. Small dormer windows here illuminate the attic, but the similar houses at Nos. 655, 663, and 665 East Pender Street (visible across the school grounds) have unbroken hipped roofs. The Gothic and Classical Revival traditions represented here co-existed throughout earlier Canadian architectural history.

LORD STRATHCONA SCHOOL   **B40**
500-Blocks Keefer and Pender Streets
Various architects, present buildings begun 1897

Opened in 1891 as the eight-room East End School, the
institution grew over the years until it became the
sprawling complex of buildings that we see today. It was
renamed Lord Strathcona School in 1900 after the C.P.R.
director who fifteen years earlier had driven home the
railway's last spike; the name eventually spread to
denote the entire area. The earliest extant portion of the
school is the red brick block on Keefer Street designed by
William Blackmore in 1897 with an imposing central
tower (unfinished inside and therefore intended for show
only) balanced by gables. The large block on Jackson
Street (designed by C. L. Morgan in 1913 but not completed until 1927) is typical of school buildings of the
period with its central block flanked by projecting wings.
The primary building on Pender Street was built in 1921
on the site of architect Thomas Hooper's original block
of 1891 and incorporates the original bricks. The gymnasium was erected about 1930. The new concrete
addition on Keefer Street (by the Gardiner Thornton
Partnership, 1972), which bears little relationship to the
earlier structures, serves as a public library and community centre.

602-622 JACKSON STREET   **B41**
Architect unknown, 1908

Attached row housing, which permits cheaper construction and maintenance costs and more advantageous use
of land, has been common in Eastern Canada but not in
the West. Here three semi-detached units are separated
by 4-foot notches. New imitation brick composition siding
covers the original clapboard.

CHINESE PUBLIC SCHOOL   **B42**
499 East Pender Street
Architect unknown, c. 1894; altered 1954

The former Jackson Avenue Baptist Church (originally
Zion Presbyterian Church), with a gabled façade and
corner tower, has been transformed into a Chinese school
with the addition of tiled flaring roofs, iron railings, and
yellow paint. As at the nearby Mon Keang School (B8),
children attend in the late afternoon after public school
classes have finished. This is the largest school of its kind
in Canada and is supported by individuals and organiza-
tions within the Chinese community.

449-459 EAST PENDER STREET **B43**
Architects unknown, 1903

These three tall and narrow shiplap houses with decorated gables, bay windows, and off-centre entrances
resemble the characteristic San Francisco row housing of
the 1870s and 1880s. Some 95 per cent of all houses built
there between 1867 and 1885 contained one or more bay
windows. Turned columns and sawn bargeboard and
brackets provide the ornamental trim in both San Francisco and Vancouver; the principal difference is that the
San Francisco detailing tends to be finer.

CHINESE UNITED CHURCH AND DORMITORY **B44**
430 Dunlevy Street
Architect(s) unknown, 1930

The United Church of Canada erected this small yellow
concrete church for Chinese Canadians. The pointed
entrance arch and windows and the wall buttresses retain
the essential elements of the traditional style, but if compared to the United Church's elaborate St. Andrew's-
Wesley (E3) built at the same time, the simplicity of the
present structure is obvious. The residential building next
door was erected for male Christian immigrants who
were encountering difficulties getting visas for their
families; today it serves as a hostel for anybody in need
of a room. The ground floor pointed arches and the
yellow paint link its design to the church.

PENDER Y.W.C.A   **B45**
375 East Pender Street
Architect unknown, 1951

This diminutive cement block and wood structure offers
social facilities to the neighbourhood. Strathcona's strong
sense of community revolves around the many secular
and religious social services located in the area.

MCLEAN PARK HOUSING PROJECT   **B46**
Blocks bounded by Jackson, Gore, Pender and Union
Streets
*Ian Maclennan (CMHC), 1962-63; Semmens and
Simpson, associated architects; David Crinion
(CMHC), 1968-70*

Urban renewal — the bulldoze and rebuild approach —
was the accepted solution for 'blighted' residential areas
in the 1950s and 1960s. Clearance in Strathcona was
begun in 1961 to make way for the McLean Park and
nearby Raymur Place (see I2) public housing projects.
The first stage of construction at McLean Park, between
Dunlevy and Jackson Streets, comprised 159 units. The
blandly modern highrise buildings contain bachelor and
one-bedroom apartments; the lower townhouses have
two- to five-bedroom suites. An additional 304 units were
built further west to Gore Street in the second stage.
Occupants — senior citizens and families alike — came
from within the Strathcona area. Under the original
plans, most of Strathcona would eventually have been
redeveloped in this way. Citizen action in this area led
the planners and the politicians to turn their attention to
the renovation of existing structures — a sounder approach sociologically and ecologically — and in 1971
the innovative Strathcona Rehabilitation Project was
born (see p. 34).

CHINESE NATIONALIST LEAGUE BUILDING **B47**
296 East Pender Street
W. E. Sproat, 1920

The Kuomintang, founded in China in 1911 and entrenched today in Taiwan as the party of Chiang Kai-shek, built this as its Western Canadian political headquarters. The building, designed by a Scottish-born architect, retains the traditional Chinese recessed balconies beneath top-floor arches; otherwise it resembles any Canadian Commercial Style building of its period.

HOTEL EAST **B48**
445 Gore Street
S. B. Birds, 1912

Like the New World Hotel in Japantown (B28), the Hotel East catered to Vancouver's newly arrived Asian immigrants. The owner was Chinese-Canadian Lee Kee. Bay windows rather than columns relieve the walls. The hotel is located at the boundary between the commercial and residential districts of Chinatown.

Eastern Business District

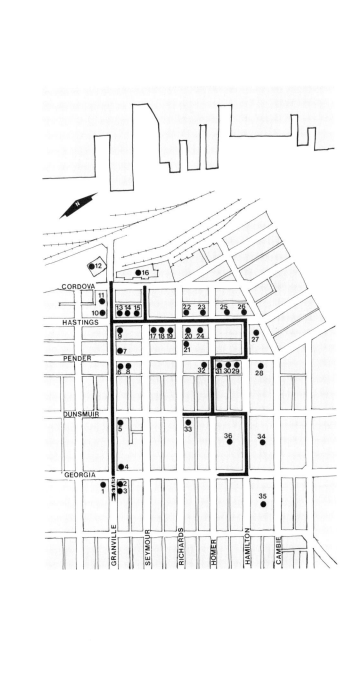

CORDOVA

11
10

13 14 15

HASTINGS

9

7

PENDER

6 8

DUNSMUIR

5

4

GEORGIA

1

2
3

12

16

22 23   25 26

17 18 19   20 24
            21

         32   31 30 29   28

                 27

33

36   34

35

GRANVILLE

SEYMOUR

RICHARDS

HOMER

HAMILTON

CAMBIE

EASTERN BUSINESS DISTRICT

In the area west of the original Granville townsite, the role of the Canadian Pacific Railway shifted from that of catalyst to a direct influence as real estate developer.

The construction of the railway across Canada was made possible by cash subsidies and land grants from the federal government. When the C.P.R. resolved to extend its rails the fourteen miles from the original terminus at Port Moody into Granville, it received an outright grant of 6,000 acres of land in the Vancouver area. The grant comprised district lot 541, the area extending west of the original townsite from Cambie to Burrard Streets and from Burrard Inlet to False Creek; all of the unsold lots in the original Granville townsite; and district lot 526, the tract extending south from False Creek to about 53rd Avenue, between Trafalgar and Ontario Streets. Private landowners in the East and West Ends further donated about one-third of their holdings to the company.

The C.P.R. first sought to establish its station and docks on the south side of English Bay at Kitsilano, but eventually decided upon the shore of Burrard Inlet west of the Granville townsite. The first station, a small wooden building at the foot of Howe Street designed by company architect T. C. Sorby, was completed only days before the arrival of the first transcontinental train on 23 May 1887.

C.P.R. Land Commissioner L. A. Hamilton began to promote the sale of land in the railway's district lot 541 as an alternative to the original townsite and the East End. Hamilton laid out the streets west of the old townsite in 1885 (he named the first one after himself and many others after prominent provincial officials) and was elected to Vancouver's first city council in 1886. To make the C.P.R. land more attractive, architect Sorby was commissioned to build the first Hotel Vancouver (see C1, D2) at the corner of Granville and Georgia Streets, today the city's principal intersection. In 1887, when the hotel was completed, Granville Street was widened from there to the station. The old Bank of British Columbia and the post office (see C18, C20, C23) were soon built in this area. In 1891 the company built an opera house behind its hotel.

Land sales followed with success. West Hastings Street became the new commercial centre of town, drawing numerous businesses away from the East End. The banks all erected their local head offices in the new area (C9, C20, C24). Many office buildings were built, and residences and churches were erected on Dunsmuir and Georgia Streets adjacent to the commercial development.

The East End (see Tour B) attracted some new construction, but soon fell far behind the rapid growth of the C.P.R.'s properties, particularly between 1908 and 1913.

The local financial crash of 1914 (see C26, C32) and the advent of war ended the boom. When building resumed in the 1920s, it centred in the area west of Granville Street.

The Eastern Business District (actually the eastern part of what is customarily called the Central Business District) remained fairly stable through the years until the late 1960s, when plans were announced for the gigantic Pacific Centre (C1) and Project 200 (C12) developments, the latter appropriately led by the C.P.R. Considerable redevelopment followed throughout the entire downtown area, and the commercial face of Vancouver is once again being drastically reshaped.

PACIFIC CENTRE   C1
S.W. Corner Georgia and Granville Streets
Victor Gruen and Associates, begun 1969; McCarter,
Nairne, and Partners, associated architects

Pacific Centre is the most ambitious superblock development in downtown Vancouver, financed by Eastern
Canadian interests with land assembly aided by the city.
Block 52 (south of Georgia), once occupied by the
C.P.R.'s old Hotel Vancouver, contains a bank tower
and a department store, both designed by Cesar Pelli of
Los Angeles. Block 42 (north of Georgia), will have two
or three tall buildings. The 19-storey I.B.M. Building was
begun in 1973 and the 20-storey Four Seasons Hotel
in 1974. The two portions of the complex will be
linked underground by a parking garage and a large
retail mall. The Toronto Dominion Tower (1969-71),
tallest in Vancouver when completed, but already
eclipsed by several newer buildings, reaches 30 storeys
above the Granville and Georgia intersection. The darkly
tinted glass curtain wall covers a steel frame, the best
Vancouver version of the influential reductive architecture of Mies van der Rohe. Structure is decoration in this
application of Mies's 'less-is-more' dictum. The vertical
rise is interrupted only by mid-height floors for mechanical equipment. This conspicuous symbol of the new face
of Vancouver has unfortunately acquired the unkind
epithet 'Black Tower.' Public reaction led to a political
decision by Mayor Arthur Phillips that the projected
fourth tower be lighter in colour. The monolithic Eaton's
Store (1970-72) contains a half-million square feet of
department store space, about the same floor area as the
Toronto Dominion office tower. The simple geometry
and blank white 'reconstituted stone' walls continue the
predilection for austerity.

BIRKS BUILDING   **C2**
718 Granville Street
Somervell and Putnam, 1912-13

This fine example of a pre-first world war office building
was erected for Montreal jewellers Henry Birks and
Sons. The 11-storey reinforced concrete frame is covered
by a handsome veneeer of white terra cotta. Decorated
spandrels are recessed behind the vertical piers, and
elegant arches grace the top. The composition is divided
into three parts, corresponding to the base, shaft, and
capital of a classical column. Three generations of Vancouverites have met their friends beneath the metal
canopy — the first permanent sidewalk canopy in Vancouver — and by the Birks Clock, which originally told
time at Granville and Hastings for Trorey Jewellers.
Despite public feeling, Birks intends to demolish this
landmark along with the adjacent Strand Theatre (p.
245) and, together with the Bank of Nova Scotia, replace
it with a large development called Vancouver Centre.

VANCOUVER BLOCK   **C3**
736 Granville Street
Parr and Fee, 1910-12

From street level to the top of its prominent clock this 14-storey 'skyscraper' stretches upward some 250 feet. Comparison with the sophisticated Birks Building (C2) reveals a relative lack of finesse. The horizontally bossed piers rise clumsily and make an awkward transition to the ornate thirteenth floor, decorated with caryatids and corner brackets. The recessed penthouse opens onto a well-used roof terrace. The frame of structural steel contrasts with the Birks Building's concrete; the two materials still compete today.

HUDSON'S BAY COMPANY STORE   **C4**
N.E. Corner Georgia and Granville Streets
Burke, Horwood, and White, 1913, 1926

Founded in Britain by royal charter in 1670 to engage in the fur trade, the Hudson's Bay Company opened up the Canadian West before government authority was established. Its base at Fort Langley, founded in 1827 some twenty miles east of today's Vancouver, was the first settlement in the lower Fraser Valley. This fine department store was the fifth outlet built by the firm in Vancouver in forty years. A sense of grandeur is imparted by the large Corinthian columns of cream terra cotta, the architectural trademark of The Bay.

JERMAINE'S STORE **C5**
600 Granville Street
Hodgson and Simmonds, 1928; McCarter and Nairne,
associated architects

As this building and the following one show, classical
ornament persisted well into the 1920s. In this structure,
originally the B.C. Electric Railway Company's show-
rooms, stone wall surfaces are relieved only by shallow
bronze window ornament and a relatively light entablature unlike the sculptural decoration of The Bay (C4) or
the integral ornament of the Birks Building (C2).

BANK OF MONTREAL **C6**
580 Granville Street
Kenneth Guscotte Rea, Inc., 1924-25

The Bank of Montreal retained the Greco-Roman temple
form after other banks had discarded it, possibly because
its venerable Roman Revival head office in Montreal was
so well known. In contrast to more robust earlier banks,
the pilasters and entablature (but not the entrance
columns) are thinly delineated. By the 1920s classical
forms were treated as decorative appliqué rather than as
integral structural elements. The banking hall is very
imposing.

ROGERS BUILDING   **C7**
470 Granville Street
Gould and Champney, 1911-12

Jonathan Rogers, the president of the Vancouver Board
of Trade, selected a prestigious Seattle firm of architects
to design this fine pre-war skyscraper. The exterior is
notable for the pink marble columns and pilasters
(marred by later ground-floor alterations) and the fine
white terra cotta walls. The upper floors were reached
by a bank of four elevators, impressive for that time even
though they were of the slow worm-gear variety.

LONDON BUILDING   **C8**
626 West Pender Street
Somervell and Putnam, 1912

The London and British North America Company
erected this 10-storey reinforced concrete structure during the wave of new office building preceding the first
world war. Like other examples of the Edwardian Commercial Style, the bottom and top portions were the
object of particular decorative efforts. The Haddington
Island stone facing is complemented by marble trim and
fine ornamental iron on the unusually tall ground-floor
portion (actually concealing the mezzanine and second
floor).

CANADIAN BANK OF COMMERCE   **C9**
640 West Hastings Street
Darling and Pearson, 1906-08

The Canadian Bank of Commerce erected the best
'temple bank' in Vancouver. Roman Ionic columns and
a rich entablature use the image of antiquity to impart a
feeling of permanence and stability. Darling and Pearson,
Toronto's leading firm of architects, demonstrated their
stylistic versatility by later participation in the design of
the Gothic Revival Parliament Buildings in Ottawa
(begun 1916).

POST OFFICE (FEDERAL BUILDING)   **C10**
701 West Hastings Street
Department of Public Works, 1905-10

This dignified essay in the Edwardian Baroque style,
with its rusticated ground floor, majestic columns, and
elegant clock tower, combines English and French architectural influences. Behind the granite façade there is an
early fireproofed steel frame. The building was occupied
for six weeks in 1938 by unemployed 'sit-downers' whose
demands for federal relief spawned violence but ultimately achieved a measure of success. The building was
relegated to the status of a branch station when the new
General Post Office was opened on Georgia Street (C36).

POST OFFICE EXTENSION   **C11**
325 Granville Street
McCarter and Nairne, 1935-39

King George VI officially opened this addition to the
Federal Building in 1939. The flat wall and emasculated
ornament indicate a sincere attempt at modernism, yet
the very use of pilasters, adopted to harmonize with the
adjacent post office, shows the continuing influence of
classicism. The building has been defaced by the new
elevated walkway to Granville Square.

GRANVILLE SQUARE   **C12**
200 Granville Street
Francis Donaldson, 1971-72

This 32-storey office tower has a more elegant (and
consequently less powerful) honeycomb façade than the
MacMillan Bloedel Building (D7) in which Donaldson
was also involved. The shaft forms the centrepiece of
Project 200, the ambitious waterfront development
financed by the C.P.R. and others (see A9). Project 200
has recently been reduced considerably in scope; one
factor influencing the changes is the growing disillusion-
ment with massive skyscraper redevelopment schemes.
The steady pedestrian traffic on the elevated plaza is
evidence of the eagerness of Vancouverites for visual
access to their waterfront. The first C.P.R. station (see
C16) stood by the tracks on the level ground below the
bluff.

ROYAL BANK BUILDING   **C13**
675 West Hastings Street
S. G. Davenport, 1929-31

The Royal Bank of Canada became the first bank in Vancouver to substitute the tall tower for the temple (contrast C9). In this it anticipated by a generation the current competition among financial institutions to express their strength through height. Designs by Eastern Canadian architects (the designer was from Montreal) continued to rely upon traditional ornament. Here the arched windows, the roofline corbels, the campanile-like asymmetrical elevator penthouse, and the detail of the elegant and spacious banking hall recall the Italian Renaissance. During modernization in 1970, the magnificent bronze entrance doors were removed and used decoratively at a new suburban branch bank in the Park Royal Shopping Centre (I36).

DAVIS CHAMBERS   **C14**
615 West Hastings Street
Dalton and Eveleigh, 1905-06

Built for lawyer E. P. Davis, this handsome office block was the first in Vancouver whose façade was systematically divided into three parts somewhat in the manner of the base, shaft, and capital of a classical column (see C2). The brick shaft features projecting courses at intervals for texture and perhaps to imitate more expensive stonework.

EMPIRE BUILDING **C15**
601 West Hastings Street
C. O. Wickenden, 1888

Dr. John Matthew Lefevre, the C.P.R. doctor and first
physician in the City Hospital, built this office block and
called it after himself. After his death it was renamed the
Empire Building. The structure was the earliest in Vancouver to reflect the commercial work of H. H. Richardson, anticipating by a decade the Richardsonian warehouses on Water Street (A14-16). Architect Wickenden
presumably encountered the Chicago-centred style during
his earlier Winnipeg practice. Attractive features of the
building are a charming internal courtyard illuminated
by a skylight and its original open-cage elevator.

C.P.R. STATION **C16**
601 West Cordova Street
Barott, Blackader, and Webster, 1912-14

The railroad station was the most self-consciously pom-
pous building type in the early years of the century. As in
New York's Pennsylvania Station (1906-10), a source of
inspiration for the columned façade, classicism is here
adopted as the most appropriate mode. Toronto's Union
Station (designed in 1913, but not completed until
1920) repeats the composition on a grander scale. The
impressive pilastered waiting room tempers its classical
dignity with paintings of Canadian landscape. Two
Vancouver stations preceded the present one. The
original simple wooden structure by T. C. Sorby (1887;
demolished c. 1949) was moved to Heatley Street with
the completion of the imposing Château style station by
Edward Maxwell (1898-99); this in turn was demolished
to make way for the present building.

TORONTO DOMINION BANK   **C17**
580 West Hastings Street
Somervell and Putnam, 1919-20

The robust columns of this post-war bank — originally
the Union Bank — are surmounted by two exposed office
floors. This building is on the site of Vancouver's second
Bank of British Columbia (by T. C. Sorby, 1887), the
first masonry building to have been erected west of Gastown. The Toronto Dominion Bank had its local head
office here until it moved into Pacific Centre (C1),
leading the geographical shift of banks from Hastings
Street to Georgia Street.

INNES-THOMPSON BLOCK   **C18**
518 West Hastings Street
C. O. Wickenden, 1889

The C.P.R. began to promote its property in this area
soon after the fire by locating its own offices at the corner
of Hastings and Richards Streets (on the site of C19).
When it lured the prestigious Bank of B.C. to this area
(see C20) rapid development followed. The present
building and the nearby Empire Building (C15), also by
architect Wickenden, are two survivors of the era. The
somewhat clumsy mixture of red brick and grey stone, of
arches and rectangles, fits our image of the pioneering
Vancouverites. The later sleek buildings on either side
bespeak the urban sophisticates of the 20th-century
metropolis.

STANDARD BUILDING   **C19**
510 West Hastings Street
Russell, Babcock, and Rice, 1913

This 15-storey structure, originally called the Weart
Building, was the highest single-slab tower in Vancouver:
only the two-stage World Building (A34) surpassed it in
height. Had the Gothic ornament at the top been
executed as elaborately as designed, it would have
reflected the fashion just being set by New York's Woolworth Building and anticipated by more than a decade
the local adoption of the mode (see D11 and 12).

BANK OF BRITISH COLUMBIA   **C20**
490 West Hastings Street
T. C. Sorby, 1889

The original Bank of British Columbia, founded in 1862
and for many years a heavy lender to the colonial
government, moved its Vancouver head office here from
its location at Hastings and Seymour (see C17). Architect Sorby chose the Italian Renaissance Revival Style,
the most imposing manner then in vogue. Pediments
covered the windows and arches lined the ground floor;
unfortunately the building has suffered badly with time.

CANADA PERMANENT BUILDING   **C21**
432 Richards Street
J. S. D. Taylor, 1911-12

The delicacy of the pilastered and pedimented façade makes these offices of the Canada Permanent Mortgage Corporation particularly pleasing. The name 'Century House' was given by a recent occupant. The present antique dealership restored the handsome interiors in 1972.

WOOLWORTH STORE   **C22**
475 West Hastings Street
Gardiner and Mercer, 1938

Woolworth's and its five-and-dime competitors filled North American cities with 2-storey buildings displaying the familiar red sign (superseded by the present blue) above the ground floor. The flat wall, the very thin relief ornament, and the elimination of the cornice on this downtown branch reveal the modernistic tendencies emerging prior to the second world war.

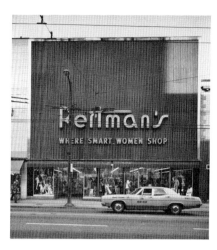

REITMAN'S STORE   **C23**
411 West Hastings Street
T. C. Sorby, 1887; altered 1960

A metal front transformed this building into a giant sign
for the women's clothier that occupies it. A number of
Vancouver retailers have chosen this manner of disguis-
ing old buildings. The present façade hides the 3-storey
McMillan Block of 1887, which contained Vancouver's
first post office until a new building was erected at Pender
and Granville Streets in 1891-92 (by C. O. Wickenden;
demolished).

ROYAL BANK OF CANADA   **C24**
404 West Hastings Street
Dalton and Eveleigh, 1903

Although emasculated in comparison to the Canadian
Bank of Commerce (C9), this former local head office
of the Royal Bank bears the distinction of being the
earliest temple bank in the city. Half-columns and pilasters enclose windows that illuminate the banking hall and
second-floor offices.

HUNTER BLOCK   **C25**
315 West Hastings Street
W. Blackmore and Son, c. 1899

High central parapets were a rule among early commercial blocks; yet this pediment is the only one in the area
to survive. Buildings of the Klondike era such as this and
the Rogers Block to the right (c. 1896) are Victorian in
the intricacy of their textured piers, broken skyline, and
projecting wall surfaces. The 4-storey Commercial Style
building to the left, built only a few years later (c. 1904,
perhaps by Parr and Fee), displays the relative simplicity
of the early twentieth century.

DOMINION BUILDING   **C26**
207 West Hastings Street
J. S. Helyer and Son, 1908-10

The Imperial Trust Company promoted this 13-storey
office tower as 'an object of pride to every citizen ...
advertising our city as the most prosperous go ahead
commercial city on the continent.' When completed as
the home of Dominion Trust Company, with whom
Imperial Trust had merged, it was described as the most
modern office building in Canada, the highest steel structure on the West Coast, and the tallest building in the
British Empire. In 1914, shortly after having sold the
building to the Dominion (now Toronto Dominion)
Bank, Dominion Trust collapsed (see C32). The red
brick and yellow terra cotta veneer is capped by a slightly
too-attenuated beaux-arts roof.

THE CENOTAPH   C27
Victory Square, Hastings and Cambie Streets
G. L. Thornton Sharp, 1924

With the erection of the stately Cenotaph, a simple
tapered granite shaft commemorating Vancouver's war
dead, the block began its second life as a civic Victory
Square. It had originally been the Court House Square,
but after the provincial government moved its courts to
Georgia Street, the court house (by T. C. Sorby and N.
Hoffar, 1888 ff) was demolished and the land used for
recruiting and revival meetings. The maple trees, planted
in 1892, survive from the court house era. In 1925
publisher Frederick Southam of the *Province* (A31)
donated money for the refurbishing of the square.

VANCOUVER VOCATIONAL INSTITUTE   C28
250 West Pender Street
Sharp and Thompson, Berwick, Pratt, 1948-49

Modern architecture was introduced to downtown Vancouver in this large building erected for the school board.
Strip windows with stucco spandrels are set off against
blank red brick walls to produce the clean lines of the
International Style, so called after its multi-national
origins. Columns are frankly exposed behind windows,
and the staircases are revealed behind sheer glass walls.
A fundamental source of the International Style was the
German Bauhaus, itself a kind of vocational school. The
old Central School and the original high school formerly
stood on the present site. The Vancouver School of Art
has long occupied the southern half of the block.

Architects Robert Berwick and C. E. Pratt joined
Sharp and Thompson in 1945 and made their firm the
most progressive in Canada.

LYRIC THEATRE   **C29**
300 West Pender Street
Architect unknown, 1906

This handsome building erected for the Lyric Theatre
and the International Order of Odd Fellows reveals the
more conservative aspect of the Richardsonian Romanesque style — conservative because its tripartite composition, heavy rusticated stonework, and rhythmic round
arches reflect traditional sources more than do commercial buildings in the style (compare A14-16). The
cornice has been lost and the entrance arch filled in with
brick during recent remodelling.

B.C. PERMANENT LOAN COMPANY   **C30**
330 West Pender Street
Hooper and Watkins, 1907

The B.C. Permanent Loan Company built the best of the
smaller temple banks. The breaking up of the façade into
a number of planes and the use of the coupled columns
is characteristic of Beaux-arts Classicism, the synthesis of
classical styles taught by the École des beaux-arts in
Paris. The Bank of Canada occupied the building between 1935 and 1966. Architects Gardiner and Mercer
accommodated the federal bank's increased cash stocks
with an enlarged vault defended by a machine-gun
emplacement. The interior contains some superb stained
glass, most notably a Tiffany-style skylight over the
central hall.

VICTORIA BLOCK   **C31**
342 West Pender Street
W. F. Gardiner, 1908

Bay windows and a central gable — mirrored on the building of the same date across the street — enlivens this stolid brick building that since its erection has contained shops, offices, and boarding rooms. The structure was connected internally to the earlier Victoria House around the corner at 514 Homer Street (1898).

WEST PENDER BUILDING   **C32**
402 West Pender Street
H. S. Griffith, 1912

The Dominion Trust Company was one of two financial firms to build this office building. The firm, which was heavily involved in providing mortgages for pre-railway British Columbians on East End real estate, was located here when it collapsed (see C26). The ornamental emphasis on bottom and top with five plain storeys between typifies the Edwardian Commercial Style. The plan allows every office to face outside with no internal light court, an important development in office-building planning. Heavy steel girders that eliminate the need for ground-floor columns allowed the owners to boast of a technological 'first.'

CATHEDRAL OF OUR LADY OF **C33**
THE HOLY ROSARY
Dunsmuir and Richards Streets
T. E. Julian and H. J. Williams, 1899-1900

Its large size, handsome design, and fine detail make
Holy Rosary Cathedral the most impressive Gothic
Revival church in Vancouver. Asymmetrical towers, the
vertical proportions, and the internal arrangement of
piers and ribbed vaults all reflect French rather than
English Gothic sources as an expression of Roman
Catholicism. Built as a parish church, Holy Rosary has
served as cathedral since 1916.

QUEEN ELIZABETH THEATRE   **C34**
Georgia and Hamilton Streets
Affleck, Desbarats, Dimakopoulos, Lebensold, Michaud, and Sise, 1957-59, 1962

Envisioning a concert hall that would form the nucleus of a multi-block civic centre in this fringe area of downtown, the city held an open competition in 1954 that attracted sixty-two entrants. The winners from Montreal, associated here for the first time, later rose to become one of Canada's leading firms of architects. Their design influenced a series of later theatre complexes across North America. The present buildings comprise a 2,835-seat concert hall, a 647-seat playhouse and recital hall (added in 1962), underground parking, a restaurant, and a public plaza. A glass and aluminum curtain wall that attempts 'to capture the timeless quality of civic building' encloses the spacious lobbies and contrasts with the solid superstructures of textured concrete. The interior is finished with warmer materials, primarily British Columbia woods.

CANADIAN BROADCASTING CORPORATION   **C35**
REGIONAL BROADCASTING CENTRE
Georgia and Hamilton Streets
C.B.C. Engineering Headquarters, begun 1973;
Thompson, Berwick, Pratt, and Partners, associated
architects

The federal government is developing two city blocks
with new buildings to centralize its local facilities. This
complex, with its distinctive angled façade, will allow the
C.B.C. to expand its western production. Across Hamilton Street, a proposed federal building (by Arthur Erickson and Associates) will provide about one million square
feet of office space — twice the capacity of Vancouver's
largest office towers. It will be suspended above the site
on four 'legs,' complying with the city planners' desire for
more ground-level open space (compare I41).

GENERAL POST OFFICE   **C36**
349 West Georgia Street
McCarter, Nairne, and Partners, Department of Public
Works, associated architects, 1953-58

Five floors covering an entire city block and three smaller
office storeys on top yield a total floor area of almost
fifteen acres. It took the largest welded steel frame in the
world to support the bulky structure and its unused
rooftop heliport. Red and grey polished granite trimmed
with a concrete border and red terra cotta spandrels
cover the frame. Special elevators carry trucks onto
various floors of the building. A 2,400-foot-long underground conveyor belt connects the post office to the
C.P.R. station (C16), but because Canadian mail went
to the air soon after completion and 'heavy' mail
switched railways, the belt was barely in operation before
it was abandoned.

Western Business District

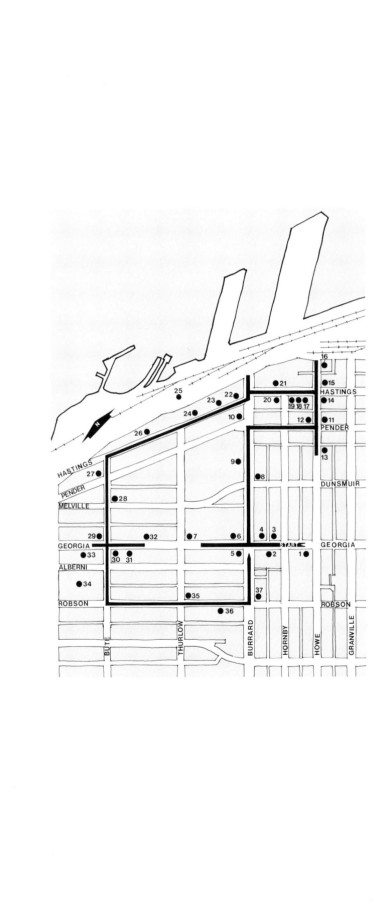

WESTERN BUSINESS DISTRICT

The Western Business District is the name given here to the commercial area located on either side of Burrard Street and north of Robson Street, the western part of today's Central Business District. The land east of Burrard formed a part of the C.P.R.'s district lot 541 (see p. 63) and the western portion belonged to the Brickmakers' Claim (p. 113). Both sections were developed by the C.P.R. beginning about 1887 as a residential district. The 1891 city directory noted that 'the West End is the home of the merchant and professional man, the East that of the lumber king and the mechanic.'

The finest early building may have been the large house on Howe Street designed by T. C. Sorby for railway superintendent Henry B. Abbott; it, like almost every other house in the area, disappeared under the subsequent commercial tide. Only two larger mansions survive, both of them south of Georgia (in the area now officially designated as the West End): Abbott's second house at 720 Jervis Street (1899) and the Evans house at 1260 West Georgia (1908; D33). Both have been divided into suites. Today the residential presence lingers in a few older apartment buildings around Georgia Street (see D29, D35) and the private clubs near the waterfront (D21, D23).

Office buildings began to appear west of Granville around 1909 with the erection of the Winch Building (D15). The newly formed stock exchange located nearby about the same time. When building activity resumed in the 1920s, the new financial and mercantile concerns epitomized by the new Stock Exchange Building (D12) and the Marine Building (D22) centred here.

The building boom of the 1960s has transformed the Western Business District. The tall towers of the Royal, Bentall, and Columbia Centres (D6, D9, D26) now dominate the skyline. Office buildings and hotels forge steadily westward, in all likelihood to be halted only by the green barrier of Stanley Park.

COURT HOUSE **D1**
800 West Georgia Street
Francis Mawson Rattenbury, 1906-12

Like so many court houses in the English-speaking world, Vancouver's Provincial Courts incorporate the columns, dome, and ornamentation of the Neoclassical Revival Style, consciously or unconsciously an attempt to associate the strength of our legal system with the authority of ancient Rome. The same pattern was followed by private finance (see C9). Architect Rattenbury, designer also of the Legislative Buildings and Empress Hotel in Victoria, created a building that is at once a beautiful monument and a positive political symbol. The marble interior with its handsome rotunda is particularly attractive. The sandstone and granite Court House was found to be too small even before its completion, and so the wing along Hornby Street was added in 1912 by Thomas Hooper. The building sits well back from Georgia Street, separated from it by the showy Centennial Fountain designed by R. H. Savery and sculpted by Count Alex von Svoboda in 1967. The Court House will probably become a new home for the Vancouver Art Gallery (D32) after the courts have moved into a new provincial government complex to be built on the two blocks behind.

HOTEL VANCOUVER   **D2**
900 West Georgia Street
Archibald and Schofield, 1928-1939

Every major city in Canada boasts its Château Style hotel
built by one of the nation's railways. The Hotel Vancouver evokes memories of medieval French castles with
its steep copper roof — now painted green — ornate
dormer windows, menacing gargoyles, and notched
'machicolations.' Left unfinished during the Depression,
the structure was rushed to completion in 1939 for the
visit of King George VI. After the C.N.R. had erected
the building to comply with an early agreement with the
city (see G22), the C.P.R. co-operatively closed its aging
rival (see C1) and lent the name 'Hotel Vancouver.'
The two railways originally managed the hotel jointly; a
decade ago Hilton Hotels assumed management and
demanded a modernization of the tradition-laden public
spaces (by Thompson, Berwick, Pratt, and Partners,
1964-68).

GEORGIA MEDICAL DENTAL BUILDING   **D3**
925 West Georgia Street
McCarter and Nairne, 1929

Many of Vancouver's physicians and dentists centralized
their practices in this 15-storey building, which contained
a hospital and auditorium, and was the first to include a
parking garage. Above the lower terra cotta facing rise
brick walls that gradually lighten in colour, terminating
in the richly ornamented cresting embellished with figures
of nurses. The elimination of classical ornament (see
D22) led its architects to boast of the design as being in
'the most modern style of architecture.'

CHRIST CHURCH CATHEDRAL   **D4**
690 Burrard Street
C. O. Wickenden, 1889-95

The oldest surviving church in Vancouver, Christ
Church was conceived in 1888 to serve the developing
West End. Funds permitted initial construction only of
the granite basement — nicknamed the 'Root House.' Six
years later the sandstone superstructure was completed.
Pointed-arched windows and wall buttresses recall the
Gothic style. The interior has fine stained glass windows
and a magnificent roof of Douglas fir. The church was
enlarged in 1909 by architects Dalton and Eveleigh, and
the chancel added in 1930 by Twizell and Twizell. Since
1929 the church has served as the cathedral of the Anglican Diocese of New Westminster. A recent attempt to
replace it with an office tower and underground sanctuary was halted in 1973 by Vancouver's city council.

BURRARD BUILDING   D5
1030 West Georgia Street
C. B. K. Van Norman and Associates, 1955-56

This 19-storey building, the first large office building erected in Vancouver after the Depression, initiated the downtown boom that continues unabated to this day. American capital financed the venture. The structure was at once the last of the old tall buildings and the first of the new. Its traditional corridor plan with staircases at either end was soon superseded by the central core system introduced at the B.C. Hydro Building (E1). On the other hand, the severely rectilinear glass, aluminum, and buff enamel curtain wall façade, whose thinness allows maximum rentable space, set the tone for most large local buildings of the next decade and a half.

ROYAL CENTRE   D6
1055 West Georgia Street
Dirassar James Jorgenson Davis, 1971-72; Webb, Zerafa, Menkes, associated architects

This emphatic addition to the Vancouver skyline includes the 38-storey Royal Bank Tower, the 720-room Hyatt Regency Hotel, a low-rise bank at the corner, and a 70-store underground shopping mall. The bulky complex has a floor space ratio of 11.84, highest among the new downtown developments. The angular corner buttresses of the office tower, which visually strengthen the otherwise anonymous façade, are in fact ventilation ducts.

MAC MILLAN BLOEDEL BUILDING   **D7**
1075 West Georgia Street
Erickson/Massey and Francis Donaldson, 1968-69

Two handsome offset towers, proportioned to eliminate interior columns, are united by a central service core. The impression of two narrow freestanding slabs has unfortunately been blocked by the Royal Centre; one must now approach from the west to gain this effect. The distinctive honeycombed façade of poured concrete may be interpreted either as a perforated wall or as a post-and-beam frame; seen either way it has sculptural strength and simplicity in keeping with what designer Arthur Erickson has called a 'Doric façade.' The tapered profile results from the progressive reduction in wall thickness from eight feet at the bottom to eight inches at the top. These load-bearing walls consume potentially rentable space, and the deep plaza reduces the floor space ratio to 9.88. The artistic merit of the design is well worth the commercial sacrifices.

YOUNG WOMEN'S CHRISTIAN ASSOCIATION   **D8**
580 Burrard Street
Vladimir Plavsic and Associates, 1967-69

Above a broad base, which contains a gymnasium, a pool, activity rooms, and offices, rise two superstructures enclosing sleeping rooms. The low-rise portion at the northern side is part of the Y.W.C.A. built in 1951 by Sharp and Thompson, Berwick, Pratt. Richly textured concrete and split travertine tile yield a warmth appropriate to the predominantly residential nature of the building.

THE BENTALL CENTRE   **D9**
Burrard Street above Pender Street
Frank W. Musson and Associates, begun 1965

Occupying some five acres, the Bentall Centre will contain four tall office towers when completed. The first two buildings, 22 and 18 storeys high, represent Vancouver's most elegant venture into high-rise design. Slender white concrete columns (actually precast panels covering poured columns) and an openwork attic surround the dark glass and bronze curtain wall. The effect is one of an attenuated classical temple. The attic provides a vertical stop to the composition, rare among newer designs although mandatory in previous eras. The 30-storey third Bentall tower, built for the Bank of Montreal (1972-73), combines the uninterrupted surface planes of the Toronto Dominion Tower (C1) with the non-structural corner piers of the Royal Bank Tower (D6). Care has been taken in designing the large plaza, which successfully attracts social activity. Its centres of attention are the bronze fountain by Seattle's George Tsutakawa and the concrete and glass branch bank that is as much sculpture as architecture. The development is named after Charles Bentall of Dominion Construction, a large local construction and development firm.

CUSTOMS BUILDING **D10**
1001 West Pender Street
C. B. K. Van Norman, 1950-54

This bulky building occupying an awkward site represents one of Vancouver's earlier large ventures into the International Style. Aluminum-framed windows alternate with granite spandrels, and the composition is framed by end piers of Haddon Island stone.

HALL BUILDING **D11**
466 Howe Street
Northwood and Chivers, 1929; McCarter and Nairne, associated architects

MONTREAL TRUST BUILDING
N.E. Corner Howe and West Pender Streets
McCarter, Nairne, and Partners, 1970

Old and new are combined in these two connected office buildings. The 10-storey Hall Building appears austere in comparison to the Stock Exchange Building across the street (D12). The white stone façade with continuous vertical piers has Gothic ornament only above the top row of windows. The new Montreal Trust building is set back from the treed sidewalk. Its concrete façade, accented with red aggregate, continues the vertical pier motif but modulates it into a rhythmic triple-bay system.

STOCK EXCHANGE BUILDING   **D12**
475 Howe Street
Townley and Matheson, 1928-29

Orange brick combines with turquoise, green, blue, and
cream terra cotta in a display of colour uncommon for
an office building. The recurrent trefoil motif and the
staccato skyline reflect the Gothic Revival, a mode made
popular for commercial structures by the Chicago
Tribune Building of 1923-25. Stockbroker S. W. Miller
planned this 10-storey building for the Vancouver Stock
Exchange (D13) and all major brokerage firms. The
exchange occupied a 'pit' reaching from basement to
second floor and entered from Pender Street. The Depression shattered Miller's hopes; he was forced to sell the
building and the exchange later moved away. Crown
Trust is now the principal tenant. In recent years massive
alterations that contrast, but harmoniously, with the old
have been executed by architects Wade, Stockdill,
Armour, and Blewett. The work is most conspicuous at
ground level where metal and glass arches have been
inserted between the original piers and a brilliant entrance hall is juxtaposed with the original ornate elevator
lobby.

VANCOUVER STOCK EXCHANGE   **D13**
536 Howe Street
McCarter and Nairne, 1953

The Vancouver Stock Exchange opened in 1907 to regulate the handling of shares, which then were being traded in taverns and bars. Since that time the Exchange has occupied eight different premises in this area, most notably the impressive Stock Exchange Building (D12). The present structure was purchased in 1964 from Canada Trust. The exterior is noteworthy only as a relatively early local exercise in the International Style; more exciting is the trading floor, which can be observed from the public gallery on the fourth storey. Vancouver's economy is so tied to Eastern finance that the exchange opens simultaneously with those in Toronto and Montreal; because of the time differential, its hours are 7 a.m. to 2 p.m.

PEMBERTON BUILDING   **D14**
744 West Hastings Street
W. M. Somervell, 1910

This brick building is ornamented at top and bottom with terra cotta in a classic example of the Edwardian Commercial Style. Wider spaces between each pair of windows reveal the location of the reinforced concrete columns. As with many of its older neighbours, the building — originally called the Bauer Building — has been brought up to date by renovation rather than redevelopment.

WINCH BUILDING   **D15**
739 West Hastings Street
Hooper and Watkins, 1908-09

R. V. Winch began the commercial development of the area west of Granville Street with this handsome office building. The arches, colonettes, and pediments and the careful attention to texture reveal architect Hooper's traditional tastes and his attention to the design of the adjacent post office (C10). The building was considered progressive rather than traditional; its fireproofed steel frame and reinforced concrete floors made it 'an entirely modern class "A" office building, the first of its kind erected in British Columbia.' The $700,000 building was one of the last to be named after the man who paid for it. Later structures generally bore the name of their corporate financers.

Winch typified the new Vancouverites who gradually gained power from the pioneer settlers. He was born in Ontario and came to Vancouver in 1886 after working on a railroad gang and as a cowboy. He made a fortune in business, principally in salmon canning and real estate. His faith in the city's developing western edge — he lived in the West End — led him to build here.

CUSTOMS EXAMINING WAREHOUSE **D16**
324 Howe Street
Department of Public Works, 1911-13

A stone base and top-floor segmental arches indicate the governmental function of this otherwise plain red brick warehouse. The building was converted into other government offices in 1958 after the completion of the new Customs building (D10).

B.C. AND YUKON CHAMBER OF MINES **D17**
840 West Hastings Street
J. C. Day, 1927

This architectural gem built for the Royal Financial Company commands attention despite its minute scale. The terra cotta façade shows a predilection for Greek ornament, as do the door frames and cresting, but permits the happy intrusion of Gothic-inspired hood mouldings above the upper windows. An interesting display of mineral samples is open to the public.

CEPERLEY ROUNSEFELL COMPANY BUILDING   **D18**
846 West Hastings Street
Sharp and Thompson, 1921

The Georgian Revival is attractively represented in this building erected by a real estate firm. Small, with brick walls and arched 'Palladian' windows that recall eighteenth-century London townhouses, the building should be compared to the same architects' grander Vancouver Club across the street (D21).

CREDIT FONCIER FRANCO-CANADIEN   **D19**
850 West Hastings Street
H. L. Stevens and Company, 1913-14

The Vancouver headquarters of a Montreal-based mortgage company is the most noble of the city's early office buildings. Its 10-storey reinforced concrete frame is sheathed in cut stone. Giant corinthian columns support a strong entablature above the second storey; pilaster strips enrich the middle floors, and the attic has graceful fluted columns and a heavy cornice with decorated cresting.

BANK OF CANADA BUILDING   **D20**
900 West Hastings Street
Thompson, Berwick, Pratt, and Partners, 1965

The Bank of Canada moved its offices to this 13-storey
building from more restricted quarters (C30). The fussy
façade of precast concrete exhibits a decorative approach
to design that consciously contrasts with the Miesian
tendency towards cool austerity (see C1). The height
and treatment of the base were determined by the
diminutive neoclassical building next door (No. 924,
originally the Hudson Bay Insurance Building, 1928).

VANCOUVER CLUB   **D21**
915 West Hastings Street
Sharp and Thompson, 1912-14

The exclusive Vancouver Club selected this site for its
first clubhouse in 1891 because of the proximity to both
the business district and the residences of its members.
This is the second building for the club on this site.
Architects G. L. T. Sharp and C. J. Thompson, English-
men recently arrived in Canada, tried to reproduce the
atmosphere of a luxurious London club. As in most
nineteenth-century English clubhouses, the window
frames and other façade ornament are inspired by the
urban palaces of the Italian Renaissance. The use of red
brick with stone trim gives the building a decidedly
English Georgian flavour. The lavish interiors include a
dining room of fine Austrian oak handcrafted by Maples
of London.

MARINE BUILDING **D22**
355 Burrard Street
McCarter and Nairne, 1929-30

Riding the crest of the Port of Vancouver's prosperous twenties, Toronto's Stimson Developers spent $2.5 million on the tallest and finest office building in the city. The architects suggested the building would bring to mind 'some great crag rising from the sea, clinging with sea flora and fauna, tinted in sea-green, touched with gold.' The brick curtain walls are heavily loaded with ornament which may seem traditional to our eyes, but the use of modernistic 'Art Deco' reliefs (named after the Parisian *Exposition des Arts Décoratifs* of 1925) rather than classical or gothic decoration (contrast C13, D12) was considered futuristic by contemporaries. The terra cotta panels depict the history of transportation and the discovery of the Pacific Coast.

The Vancouver Merchants Exchange and other shipping groups became the principal tenants. Shortly after completion, the Depression broke the developers. They offered the building to Vancouver as a city hall; when city legislators refused to pay $1 million, Britain's Guinness interests acquired it for less. Despite its age and the erection of numerous new office towers, the Marine Building has successfully retained many of its original tenants, including the firm of architects that designed it.

UNIVERSITY CLUB   **D23**
1021 West Hastings Street
Architect unknown, 1929

Built by the Quadra Club, the building went through a
number of owners before being bought in 1957 by the
University Club. Arches, the patterned brickwork, and
decorated colonnettes add Renaissance flavour.

GUINNESS TOWER   **D24**
1055 West Hastings Street
Charles Paine, 1967-69

Glass and green enamel rectangles separated by aluminum strips produce the polished geometrical look introduced to Vancouver more than a decade earlier by the
Burrard Building (D5). The Guinness Tower covers the
approximate site of the Three Greenhorns' first cabin
(see p. 113), probably the first house to have been
erected on Burrard Inlet. This 23-storey building and its
neighbours to the west offer their tenants fine panoramas,
but obstruct the view of many other Vancouverites.

IMMIGRATION BUILDING **D25**
Foot of Thurlow Street
E. E. Blackmore for the Department of Public Works,
1914-15

Seen best from the plaza of the Guinness Tower, this
building with its sheer orange brick walls and pigeon-
covered châteauesque hipped roof was new arrivals' first
introduction to Vancouver. Countless reinforced concrete and steel sheet pilings keep the structure from
slipping into Burrard Inlet. Prejudices of the era emerge
in the provision of separate dining rooms and dormi-
tories for 'White' and 'Chinese' immigrants. To the left
can be seen the entrance to the C.P.R. tunnel (1931)
that leads to the main yards on False Creek (see G1).

COLUMBIA CENTRE **D26**
1111 - 1177 West Hastings Street
Waisman Architectural Group, begun 1965

This complex contains the 13-storey Baxter Building
(1965), the 27-storey Board of Trade Tower (1968), the
new Harbour-Side Vancouver Holiday Inn between
them (begun 1972), and a lower office building at the
western end of the site (begun 1973). The Baxter Building alternates square concrete columns painted dark grey
with circular colonettes, which are in fact hollow ventilation ducts. This unusual detail was refined in the second
tower.

EAST ASIATIC HOUSE   **D27**
1201 West Pender Street
Gerald Hamilton and Associates, 1963

A picturesque group of three delicately detailed blocks, one low and two of moderate height, is substituted for the more common slab tower. White reconstituted marble wall panels (shaped to enclose the building's mechanical services) float above the dark green arches of the ground floor.

MOORE OFFICE   **D28**
626 Bute Street
McCarter, Nairne, and Partners, 1968

In this modest custom office for Moore Business Forms, designer Blair MacDonald chose not to compete with the architecturally unexciting neighbourhood. The corner of the site has been planted and left as public open space. General offices occupy the area behind the diagonal southwestern wall, the windows deeply recessed behind protective sun breaks. Executive offices face the scenic northern view. The frank exposure of sandblasted poured concrete and the expression of the wall thickness acknowledge the architecture of Le Corbusier and the bulky Brutalist Style, but these sources are tempered here by crisp edges and delicately proportioned walls.

THE BANFF **D29**
1201 West Georgia Street
H. B. Watson, 1909

The two apartment blocks and the house occupying this block of Bute Street remind us that the area was once entirely residential. The brick walls of the Banff (now painted white) are variously relieved by bay windows, arches, and balconies. Typical of early apartments, the site is almost completely covered; only a 7-foot alley along part of the western wall, guaranteeing some light to its windows, is left undeveloped. The floor space ratio is close to 4, higher than any of the new high-rise apartment buildings in the West End (see E11).

VOLKSWAGEN PACIFIC BUILDING **D30**
1190 West Georgia Street
Architect unknown, 1925

This 3-storey showroom and garage built for Willis-Kingsley Motors and since occupied by a number of other automobile dealers is an early example of an exposed reinforced concrete building. Concrete had been used in Vancouver for taller structures for almost twenty years (see A1), but always received a veneer of stone, brick, or terra cotta. The commercial and quasi-industrial nature of this building permitted the use of exposed concrete. Because Vancouver had no zoning legislation until 1927, this stretch of Georgia Street contains a hodge-podge of building uses.

FIRST CHURCH OF CHRIST, SCIENTIST   **D31**
1160 West Georgia Street
Matheson and Du Gleere, 1918

Christian Science has always preferred classically derived architectural forms. This brick church featuring delicate arches looks back to the classicism of Georgian England for inspiration.

VANCOUVER ART GALLERY   **D32**
1145 West Georgia Street
Sharp and Thompson, 1931; Ross A. Lort, 1949-51

The Vancouver Art Gallery opened in October 1931 following an organizational campaign led by local arts patron Harry A. Stone. The gallery tripled in size in 1951 after being bequeathed a large collection of paintings by local artist Emily Carr. Architect Lort added the central and eastern galleries and erected a distinctive new façade across the entire structure. Two large concrete surfaces are bordered by windows, punctuated by vertical slabs, and covered by a curved overhanging roof. In recent years the gallery has taken to painting the exterior wall of the right-hand portion in a bright colour (recently orange, yellow, and then covered in leopard spots).

W. GEORGE EVANS HOUSE   **D33**
1260 West Georgia Street
Architect unknown, 1908

Insurance executive W. G. Evans built this well-main-
tained clapboard and shingle house. It is one of the last
two surviving houses from 'Blueblood Alley,' the area
first developed as the residential enclave of the C.P.R.
officials. The only other remaining house was the residence of C.P.R.'s general superintendent Henry B.
Abbott (720 Jervis Street, 1899). Both homes have been
converted into suites.

PACIFIC PALISADES   **D34**
Bute to Jervis Streets between Alberni and Robson
Streets
Bing Marr and Associates, 1966-69

Two 22-storey apartment buildings, a 20-storey hotel
with ground-floor stores, and a 5-storey office building
surround a landscaped plaza. Warm brown colours are
dominant: glass, insulated glass sandwich panels, and
anodized aluminum cover the administration block, and
dash stucco aggregate panels cover the towers. Delicate
white arches allow a relatively unobstructed view at
ground level. The complex shares the block with the
forceful Blue Horizon Hotel (Lort and Lort, 1967). The
office building at 747 Bute Street is a characteristic
example of the New Formalism. The style, a kind of new
Neoclassical Revival, is a decorative offshoot of Miesian
architecture and the International Style that sacrifices
structural rationalism for delicate visual delight.

MANHATTAN APARTMENTS   **D35**
784 Thurlow Street
Parr and Fee, 1908

Built for industrialist W. L. Tait (see F19), the Manhattan was one of the earliest apartment blocks in the
city as well as the first to be built on a new plan with
high site coverage and a deep courtyard for light. Its
name foreshadowed the area's future 'Manhattaniza-
tion,' and it formed the model for countless later apartment buildings. The bay windows, contrasting to the
customary plain wall surfaces of Parr and Fee's commercial buildings, provide a sense of residential dignity, as
do the ornate columns and balcony of the recessed
entranceway.

   The earliest apartment building in the city was Merrill
(or Haro) Mansions a block away at Haro and Thurlow
Streets, built in 1907 and demolished in 1972. It was
designed somewhat as an oversized gabled wooden house.

1000-BLOCK ROBSON STREET   **D36**
Various architects and dates

The laying of streetcar tracks in 1899 determined the
commercial nature of Robson Street. The retail centre of
Vancouver's German community, the street is popularly
known as Robsonstrasse. The import stores and delicates-
sens may be undistinguished architecturally, but their
continental wares and foods attract some of the heaviest
foot traffic in the city. Attempts to convert this and other
streets to partial or full pedestrian malls are under
consideration.

VANCOUVER PUBLIC LIBRARY   **D37**
750 Burrard Street
Semmens and Simpson, 1956-57

This successor to the Carnegie Library (B14) is the
administrative centre of the city's large library system,
the central book collection and reference library, and a
downtown lending branch. Librarians across Canada
were consulted to aid in the design. A reinforced concrete
structure with wide column spacing allows clear interior
spaces and flexibility for changes and expansion. On the
exterior, glass and coloured stone are combined into a
handsome pattern that distinguishes between offices,
stacks, and reading rooms. Large areas of glass invite
passers-by to enter and become library users.

Walking Tour   E

The West End

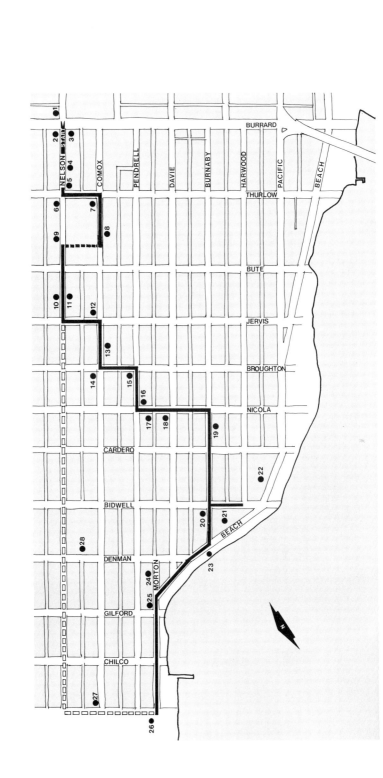

THE WEST END

Coal and clay, two rather unglamorous mineral resources, were the lures that attracted settlers to the West End of Vancouver. In the summer of 1859, the survey ship H.M.S. *Plumper* found coal on the shore of Burrard Inlet near the foot of Bute Street. Coal Harbour was never mined actively, but the discovery led a young English potter named John Morton to search for clay for brickmaking. In 1862, Morton, his cousin Samuel Brighouse, and friend William Hailstone pre-empted the 'Brickmaker's Claim,' the entire 550-acre parcel of land between Burrard Inlet and English Bay from Burrard Street to Stanley Park. The 'Three Greenhorns,' as they were called (commemorated only in the name of a local restaurant), took possession of the whole of today's West End for about one dollar per acre; little did they realize that after their time it would become some of the most valuable real estate in Canada.

Brickmaking proved unprofitable. The Greenhorns abandoned Vancouver in 1864 and stayed away for almost two decades. Brighouse acquired large holdings in the Fraser River delta; his name survives as a part of suburban Richmond. In 1882 they returned to Burrard Inlet and tried without success to promote land sales in the eastern part of their land, nostalgically named the City of Liverpool. Two years later they were persuaded to give one-third of their land to the C.P.R. as part of the railroad's land grant.

The first concerted settlement of the West End came in 1887, when the C.P.R. began to develop Georgia Street west of Burrard as a residential area (see p. 87). 'Blueblood Alley' set the tone for subsequent West End settlement. The tree-lined streets soon contained many fine homes. The southern shore at English Bay (E23) became a fashionable beach, and beautiful Stanley Park (E26) formed the western boundary. The West End became the choice residential area of Vancouver's moneyed elite (many of whom had moved from Eastern Canada).

Shortly after 1900 the situation changed. Duplexes and apartments began to appear among the houses. Commercial development occurred, principally along the streetcar lines on Davie, Denman, and Robson Streets. Wealthier families began to move to Shaughnessy Heights (Tour F). Some larger homes were converted into rooming houses or suites; others were demolished to make way for more apartment buildings. The West End was finished as a single-family residential area.

In the 1920s the city fathers recognized the dangers of allowing development to proceed without controls. A town planning commission was established to recommend guidelines and prepare a master plan. The commission, in turn, appointed Harland Bartholomew and Associates of St. Louis, Missouri, as consultants. The result of their efforts was the city's first zoning by-law, enacted in 1927 to place controls upon land use, density, and building size. Construction in the West End was restricted to residential buildings of 6 storeys except for buildings intended for commercial use on Davie, Denman, and Robson Streets.

Pressures for development increased after the second world war. The city's expanding commercial district encroached upon the West End in 1955, when the tall B.C. Electric Building at Nelson and Burrard (E1) was built. In the following year the city's planners rewrote the zoning by-law and raised the building height limit within the West End residential district to allow tall construction in return for lower site coverage. Developers responded by creating the forest of high-rises that, for better or for worse, has given Vancouver its dramatic skyline. Another important zoning change, passed in 1964, encouraged the construction of larger balconies for better outdoor access (see E19).

Nobody anticipated the speed with which the old West End would be obliterated; today hardly a block survives without one or more large buildings dominating its predecessors. The West End has been claimed as the most densely populated area in Canada. So alarming has been the increase in population and the depersonalization that late in 1972 Vancouver's planners offered a new scheme to reduce West End density. The effects of the proposals must be awaited; perhaps they have not come too late.

Because of its length, this tour does not follow a circular route. Cycling enthusiasts can make the tour and return in style. If you are uncertain of your stamina, arrange to be met by car at the end of the tour or take the bus at Denman Street. Confirmed pedestrians should proceed along the edge of Stanley Park and back along Nelson Street as indicated in the map. The popcorn vendors who patrol the sidewalks along English Bay offer light refreshments; Denman Street from Nelson to the beach is lined with a number of small but surprisingly good restaurants, some serving beer and wine.

B.C. HYDRO BUILDING   **E1**
970 Burrard Street
Thompson, Berwick, and Pratt, 1955-57

The B.C. Electric Company moved here from Gastown
(A38) after erecting the first tall building south of
Georgia Street. The company was taken over by the
provincial government in 1961-62 and renamed B.C.
Hydro. A distinctive tapered plan allows every desk to be
no farther than 15 feet from a window. A porcelain and
glass curtain wall conceals an innovative structure in
which floors are cantilevered from a bearing central service core like branches from a tree and supported only
slightly by slender perimeter columns. Prominent local
artist B.C. Binning designed the mosaic of blue, green,
and black tile. The low adjacent Dal Grauer Substation
(by Sharp and Thompson, Berwick, Pratt, 1953-54),
whose mechanical works are exposed behind a glass wall,
introduced modernity into the traditional West End.

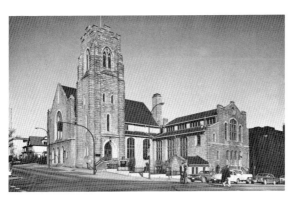

FIRST BAPTIST CHURCH   **E2**
969 Burrard Street
Burke, Horwood, and White, 1910-11

A monumental façade of cut stone flanked by a stately
bell tower introduces the later phase of the Gothic
Revival to Vancouver church architecture. It may be
contrasted to the lesser scale of earlier Christ Church
Cathedral (D4). The spacious sanctuary, handsomely
fitted with a fine wooden coffered ceiling and balconies,
was rebuilt after a fire in 1931. An education wing to the
north contains classrooms, offices, and social halls.

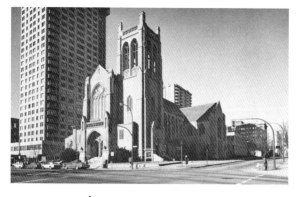

ST. ANDREW'S-WESLEY UNITED CHURCH **E3**
1012 Nelson Street
Twizell and Twizell, 1931-33

The English-born architects Robert Percival and George Sterling Twizell excelled in building traditional churches. The granite façade, with a superbly rich stained glass window by Gabriele Loire of Chartres, France (1969), towers 109 feet above Burrard Street. Inside, a high timber trussed roof covers the large aisled nave with its Gothic arcade and clerestory. Reinforced concrete is used throughout but never permitted to show; stone conceals the material outside and a special stone-like finish disguises it within.

CAROLINE COURT **E4**
1058 Nelson Street
R. M. Matheson, 1912

By 1912, when this 70-suite patterned brick building was erected, such buildings had become commonplace in the West End. Site coverage is high with only a narrow strip left along each side for internal illumination. Its 7 storeys give it a floor space ratio of about 6, almost twice the maximum now permitted for West End apartments.

1070-72 AND 1074-76 NELSON STREET   **E5**
Architects unknown, 1903

Duplexes such as these marked the beginning of multiple-family residences in the West End. These two frame dwellings were erected at the same time, although to different designs. Both have shiplap siding on the ground floor and shingles in the gabled second storey; such combinations were characteristic of early Vancouver houses. The duplexes are built right to the property line so that their side eaves nearly touch.

NICHOLSON TOWER   **E6**
1115 Nelson Street
Erickson/Massey, 1968-69

This elegant tower by designer Ken Burroughs was financed jointly by the federal and provincial governments to provide 223 dwelling units for senior citizens. The project is named after former Lieutenant-Governor John R. Nicholson, who as a federal cabinet minister had been instrumental in conceiving the project. Central Mortgage and Housing Corporation set the programme requirements and accepted the development proposal of Frank Stanzl Construction Ltd., who selected the architects. Concrete bearing walls support the structure on the narrow east and west sides, and a screen wall of brick, glass, and concrete fills in the other two sides. The building is divided into individual suites; common rooms are located only on four floors. The result differs little from any tall residential high-rise; one wonders whether the elderly would not be served better by a building designed to meet their special needs.

1025 AND 1037 THURLOW STREET **E7**
Architect unknown, 1901

These two survivors of a group of four smaller houses
were built for families of modest incomes. These asymmetrical buildings are typical of the design of the time.
Shiplap is used as the primary sheathing, while narrower
boards are applied decoratively at various angles. The
gable peak features scalloped shingles, and carved pin-
wheel trim decorates the bay window. Wood, the most
ubiquitous building material on the West Coast, was —
and is — handled particularly well by architects and
builders in British Columbia.

1100-BLOCK COMOX STREET   E8
Various architects, c. 1903-12

The typical Vancouver middle-class dwelling house of the first decade of the century was a timber building two and one-half storeys high with a gable end presented to the street, a covered porch, and one or more bay windows on the façade. The type, a slightly later development of the houses seen in B38 and B42, combines the broad proportions of the gabled and verandahed Southern Ontario city house (usually of brick in the East) with the bay windows and varied wood facing of the picturesque row house of San Francisco. Such dwellings may have been common throughout the city, but they *were* the West End. By the outbreak of the first world war virtually every West End street was lined with such buildings. This is one of the few blocks to remain virtually intact; another is the 1000-block of Pacific Street.

Most such houses were designed and built separately or in small groups by minor speculative developers. Three who worked on this block were T. J. Lightheart, J. P. Matheson, and Benjamin Williscroft. Variants occur in proportions, type of wood siding, porch supports, number of bay windows, and in the occasional adoption of corner turrets, but the fundamentals remain constant. Today most are rooming houses. A number have been covered with stucco or with asbestos shingles.

NELSON COURT　　　　　　　　　　　　　　　　**E9**
1147 Nelson Street
Grant and Henderson, 1909

Balconies perforated with quatrefoils lend a vaguely
Gothic air to this early apartment block. Its brick façade
conceals a structural timber frame. The lobby is designed
much like the hall of a private home, with a large staircase rising from its centre. The mature boulevard trees
(mostly horse chestnuts) reveal the care with which the
West End was landscaped.

EDWARDIAN AND TWEEDSMUIR　　　　　　　　**E10**
APARTMENTS
1235 and 1245 Nelson Street
Architect(s) unknown, 1931

Originally the Queen Anne Gardens, this pair of apartment houses has lower site coverage than earlier buildings
(see E4). The buildings have the brick piers, decorated
spandrels, and broken skyline of contemporaneous office
buildings (compare D12), used here with a crisp neat-
ness that looks surprisingly modern.

HARLEY HOUSE AND SUTTON PLACE   **E11**
1230 and 1260 Nelson Street
Erickson/Massey, 1970

Little more than a generation separates these two apartment towers from their earlier counterparts across the
street (E10); yet the difference is astounding. Broad
3-storey walk-ups have been superseded by 20-storey
towers that cover only a small fraction of their site. The
floor space ratio is about 3, hardly more than that of the
Edwardian and Tweedsmuir Apartments, and considerably lower than many pre-1930 apartment buildings
(compare E4). Poured concrete is boldly sculpted into a
strong relief composition; balconies and moulded spandrels are exploited for powerful effect. Matthew Court
(by Wilfred D. Buttjes and Associates, 1972-73), located
across Jervis Street, is similar in design.

MARINA MANOR   **E12**
1050 Jervis Street
Architect unknown, 1956

During the 1950s many austere 3-storey walk-up apartments were built in the West End. Three floors (and a
penthouse) were the maximum permitted in inexpensive
wood frame construction. The Marina Manor is characteristic with its pink and cream roughcast stucco walls
and horizontal plate glass windows that may have
appeared starkly modern in their time but look barren
today.

ERKINDALE AND ELIZABETH APARTMENTS **E13**
1300-Block Comox Street
Architects unknown, 1907-11

In the early 1960s speculator Alexander Di Cimbriani
began to purchase West End houses, and to restore, reno-
vate, and rent them to 'quiet, refined tenants.' Today
about two dozen buildings display the distinctive white
stucco walls with black trim. The 1300-block on Comox
Street contains some ten immaculate frame houses from
the period 1907 to 1911, the only large and healthy
rehabilitated group in the West End. The block also has
a more substantial house designed in 1901 for broker and
lumberman Herbert G. Ross by Samuel Maclure (1345
Comox), a frame apartment building of 1923 by A. E.
Henderson (formerly the Sheffield Apartments, 1325
Comox), and a newer (1942) brick apartment building
(formerly the Vincent Apartments, 1375 Comox). A new
townhouse apartment block at 1300 Comox that pre-
serves the character of the street was designed for the
Di Cimbriani company in 1972 by Thompson, Berwick,
Pratt, and Partners.

ST. JOHN'S UNITED CHURCH **E14**
1401 Comox Street
John J. Honeyman, 1906

This Gothic Revival church fits its corner site well with
a tall tower inserted between two gabled façades. The
interior has an unusual curved balcony and a fine timber
roof. Architect Honeyman, perhaps a kinsman of the
talented Glasgow architect of the same name, practised
in Nanaimo and Rossland before reaching Vancouver.

THOMAS A. FEE HOUSE **E15**
1119 Broughton Street
Parr and Fee, 1904

This turreted house, originally occupied by architect Fee,
is typical of the larger homes of wealthier Vancouverites.
The hipped roof with a deck retains a trace of its original
iron cresting. Very few of these larger West End houses
remain; those that do are invariably multiple dwellings
— this one has been renamed Holly Manor. Thomas Fee
was born in Eastern Canada and trained briefly as an
architect in Minneapolis. He was an active developer as
well as an architect; Granville Street's many white glazed
brick hotels and commercial buildings are the products
of his dual role.

THE BEAUFORT **E16**
1160 Nicola Street
Architect unknown, 1932

The Tudor fad, so popular two decades earlier for private homes, continues in this 3-storey apartment block.
Artificial stone, brick, and decorative half-timbering
combine handsomely in front; plain stucco covers the
rear. One of the best buildings in the mode is Tudor
Manor at 1311 Beach Avenue (by Townley and Matheson, 1927).

B. T. ROGERS COACH HOUSE　　　　　　　　　**E17**
1155 Nicola Street
Probably by Samuel Maclure, c. 1901

ANGUS SERVICE GARAGE
1155 Nicola Street
Architect unknown, 1935

A small half-timbered gasoline station and rows of parking garages (former stables that were enlarged as cars grew longer) stand in front of the original coach house of B. T. Rogers' adjacent 'Gabriola' (E18). A broad roof with bracketed bellcast eaves covers the clapboard walls of the handsome coach house.

B. T. ROGERS HOUSE ('GABRIOLA')　　　　　**E18**
1531 Davie Street
Samuel Maclure, 1900-01

Samuel Maclure, the best residential architect of his time in British Columbia, built this superb mansion for sugar king B. T. Rogers (see I3). The richly textured stone comes from nearby Gabriola Island. The blocky massing gains picturesque flavour through the asymmetry, tall chimneys, and circular gazebo. The fine wood-panelled interiors feature eighteen fireplaces, and the concrete basement was the earliest in Vancouver. The house is now an apartment building connected to the brick Angus Apartments (1924) to the west.

1500- AND 1600-BLOCKS BURNABY STREET **E19**
Various architects and dates

Within this attractive two-block stretch of Burnaby
street one can trace the recent development of apartment building design in the West End. The 1500-block
contains an assortment of modest apartments. The oldest
is a house that has been converted into suites (1554
Burnaby, 1908). The numerous 3-storey apartment blocks
retain the smaller scale; most are unrelieved stucco boxes
(such as the Laguna Beach Apartments, 1516 Burnaby,
1957), but they include a newer balconied building of
the sixties (the Mivic Apartments, 1540 Burnaby, 1968).
The 9-storey El Presidente (1521 Burnaby, 1965) is the
only taller building in the group. The 1600-block is closer
to the beach; its land is therefore more expensive and
more densely developed. Kevin Manor (1661 Burnaby,
1962), with its façade of ceramic tile, has very narrow
balconies because at the time of its construction balconies
were included in the calculation of the floor space ratio.
When balconies were omitted from the computed floor
area in 1964, architects responded by increasing their
size. The difference is evident in the large balconies of
the 13-storey Heather House (1650 Burnaby, 1966) and
the 21-storey Surf Crest (1251 Cardero, 1965). The
mature birch trees along the boulevards do much to tie
the varied buildings together.

THE IMPERIAL APARTMENTS   **E20**
1255 Bidwell Street
Peter Kaffka, 1962-63

Promoted at its opening as the tallest building in Western
Canada, this apartment block with its bland white stucco
walls stretching some 30 storeys high was developed by
former mayor Thomas Campbell. Its 266 single-bedroom
suites contributed to the assault on family living that has
characterized new apartments in the West End.

ALEXANDRA PARK BANDSTAND   **E21**
Beach Avenue between Burnaby and Harwood Streets
Architect unknown, 1914

An octagonal bandstand, whose two-tiered roof is supported by remarkable scroll brackets, occupies the centre
of a charming small triangular park named after Edward
VII's queen. By the Beach Avenue entrance to the park
is a marble water fountain with a bronze plaque (by
sculptor Charles Marega) commemorating Joe Fortes,
the black lifeguard who taught countless Vancouver
children to swim at English Bay.

BEACH TOWERS   **E22**
1600-Block Beach Avenue
C. B. K. Van Norman and Associates, 1964-65; 1968

Three cruciform reinforced concrete towers incorporate several design innovations including large balconies (see E19). The developers, Block Bros. Realty, planned the complex to appeal to childless tenants by designing most of the 450 suites as single-bedroom or studio apartments. A fourth tower was added north of Harwood Street.

ENGLISH BAY BEACH   **E23**
Beach Avenue

English Bay became a popular swimming beach with the development of the West End in the 1890s. The city recognized the potential value of a continuous public beach and bought most of the waterfront properties between 1902 and 1911. The last property to be acquired was Engelsea Lodge (1913) at 2046 Beach Avenue, which was purchased in 1967 and is scheduled for demolition in 1977. A bath house and a large pier were built about 1909 but they were replaced by the present undistinguished public facilities in 1931. The original beach surface of broken quartz has been covered with sand dredged from the bottom of the bay. As recently as 1962 raw sewage from Vancouver and the North Shore forced the closure of English Bay to swimmers; new minimal sewage treatment plants have rendered pollution levels tolerably low. Sailboats complement the scenic beauty and large freighters anchor in the bay while awaiting dock space in Vancouver harbour.

OCEAN TOWERS   **E24**
1835 Morton Street
Rix Reinecke, 1957-58

When proposed in early 1956, this 18-storey apartment
building exceeded the maximum size permitted under
zoning regulations (as did the B.C. Hydro Building, E1).
The City Planning Department and the Town Planning
Commission opposed the building because it would block
the view of the water, but city council empowered itself
to approve such non-conforming applications. The result
was the first tall building along English Bay. The building
subsequently became one of the first to convert to ownership of suites by individual tenants, anticipating the
legislative establishment of condominiums under the
provincial Strata Titles Act of 1966.

SYLVIA HOTEL   **E25**
1154 Gilford Street
W. P. White, 1912

Built as the 70-suite Sylvia Court Apartments, the building formerly commanded high rents. The Depression
forced its conversion into a hotel, best known for its top-
floor Sky Room Restaurant ('Dine in the sky at the
Sylvia') that was moved to ground level in 1965. The
brick walls have a stone and terra cotta base and cap.
The particularly fine frieze and cornice turn around the
corner and stop; the eastern wall is faced in cheaper
brick. In the phrase of her day, the Sylvia has a 'Queen
Anne front and a Mary Ann back.'

BOARD OF PARKS AND PUBLIC RECREATION   **E26**
2099 Beach Avenue, Stanley Park
Underwood, McKinley, and Cameron, 1960

The park board's handsome offices use granite, wood, and shrubbery in a low asymmetrical design that fits well into the park landscape. Inside, the exposed Douglas fir structural members and panelled walls of cedar and Japanese ash combine in an exciting two-levelled space. Architect Percy Underwood designed the furniture, light fixtures, and other fittings. The building stands by the Beach Avenue entrance to 1,000-acre Stanley Park, the magnificent park leased by the city in 1886 (at the urging of city alderman and C.P.R. land commissioner L. A. Hamilton) and named after the Governor General, Lord Stanley of Preston. The peninsula had long been the site of native settlements. It now contains recreational facilities, a zoo and a fine aquarium, swimming beaches, and miles of forested roadways and paths.

The tour ends at this point. Two buildings are appended for those who return on foot.

2075 COMOX STREET   **E27**
Wilfred D. Buttjes and Associates, 1968

This 22-storey apartment building commanding a fine
view of Stanley Park is one of the most handsome in the
West End, with effective use of textured concrete and
cantilevered balconies.

DENMAN PLACE   **E28**
1733 Comox Street
Wilding and Jones, J. A. Murray, associated architects,
1968-69

A 32-storey tower of sculpted reinforced concrete (originally intended to rise 48 floors) tops a commercial complex. The low base encloses a shopping mall, a supermarket, restaurants, a cinema, and two parking garages,
while the tower accommodates a hotel and apartments.
At the time the site had to be rezoned to allow the
development; proposed new area zoning may encourage
this kind of healthy mixture of uses.

Shaughnessy Heights

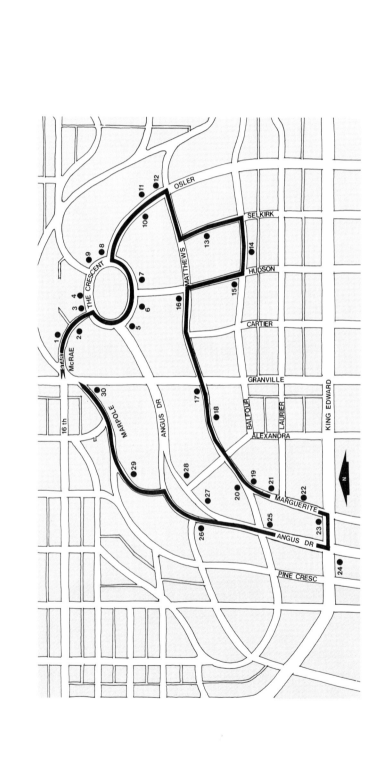

SHAUGHNESSY HEIGHTS

The Canadian Pacific Railway announced in 1907 that a 250-acre portion of its immense land holdings south of False Creek would be cleared and developed as an exclusive residential area. Strategically located on the crest of a hill, the subdivision was to be named Shaughnessy Heights after C.P.R. president Sir Thomas Shaughnessy.

The timing was perfect. With the city's economic prosperity, the opening in 1909 of a new Granville Street Bridge, and the proliferation of apartment building in the West End, people were eager to move to the development.

Shaughnessy Heights was laid out by the Danish engineer L. E. Davick and the Montreal landscape architect F. Todd with tree-lined streets and boulevards that curve along the natural contours of the land. Many of the streets — Angus, Marpole, Osler, Hosmer, Nanton among others — were named after C.P.R. officials. The area was subdivided into lots that varied in size from one-fifth of an acre to one and one-half acres. The railway set $6,000 as the minimum price of any house built and offered generous loans to encourage building.

The first lots were sold in 1909. After two more years of stump-clearing and another of road building, fine homes began to appear throughout the area. Within two decades virtually every influential family in Vancouver had moved to Shaughnessy Heights. In 1922 the provincial government passed the Shaughnessy Heights Building Restriction Act, limiting the area to single-family homes and discouraging the further division of properties. Second and third Shaughnessy subdivisions extended development south to 41st Avenue, but the newer areas never achieved the exclusiveness of the original section.

The depression of the thirties and the second world war hurt the area badly. Residents could no longer afford to maintain expensive homes, and houses stood empty and deteriorating in a time of severe housing shortage. Emergency wartime legislation was passed to permit the conversion of such residences into rooming houses. All shared homes operating in 1955 were permitted by law to remain that way, but new rental suites are still banned. The restrictions against multiple-family dwellings and further subdivision have eliminated most pressures for redevelopment. The provincial legislation was repealed by the B.C. government in 1971, but Shaughnessy Heights is still protected by the city's strict RS-4 single-family-dwelling zoning schedule (implemented in 1959).

Subdivisions are possible (see F1, F18, F28, and F29), but new lots are supposed to be at least 85 feet wide and 9,500 square feet in area.

The tour of Shaughnessy Heights begins at Granville Street and 16th Avenue, the limit of the South Granville shopping area (known particularly for its antique shops). The Hycroft Medical Building and the Hycroft Towers mark the boundary between the commercial-apartment area and residential Shaughnessy Heights. The hill rises sharply and permits a fine view of the water and mountains over the tops of all but the tallest buildings.

MCRAE HOUSE ('HYCROFT') **F1**
1489 McRae Avenue
Somervell and Putnam, 1909-13

General Alexander Duncan McRae, a future senator
with interests in lumbering, fisheries, coal, and real estate,
chose a site with a superb view for his early mansion. Six
majestic columns support a grand *porte-cochère*. The
rest of the façade is equally imposing but somewhat
disappointing in detail; windows and balconies of various
sizes and shapes barely hold the composition together.
The large basement ballroom with its mirrored bar is
reached directly from the main entrance. The house was
given to the federal government during the second world
war for use as a veterans' hospital. Since 1962 it has
been the home of the University Women's Club. The fine
interiors, with their rich plasterwork decoration by
Charles Marega, have been well restored. Most of the
outbuildings and gardens east of the house have been
replaced by a townhouse development (by Gerald Hamilton and Associates, 1963) for which a special zoning
change was obtained.

WALTER C. NICHOL HOUSE   **F2**
1402 The Crescent
Maclure and Fox, 1912-13

Its English ancestry and picturesque appearance made
the half-timbered Tudor Revival the favourite mode in
Shaughnessy Heights. This superb house for *Province*
publisher (and later Lieutenant-Governor) Nichol retains
its formality despite asymmetry. The vertical strips of
cedar and stucco alternating on the upper wall are
relieved by stone and shingle at the base and corners.
The voluminous roofs with broad eaves and tall chimneys are typical of houses by talented Samuel Maclure,
who later built 'Miraloma' for Nichol in Sidney, B.C.
The emphatic horizontal roof line relates the building to
its site in a manner that corresponds to the prairie houses
of Frank Lloyd Wright.

H. E. RIDLEY HOUSE   **F3**
1389 The Crescent
Probably by J. A. Benzie, c. 1911

The combination of half-timbering, shingles, and stone
seen in the previous house are incorporated here into a
composition fragmented by gables, bay windows, and the
porte-cochère. The lack of unity is nevertheless attractive
in its variety.

On The Crescent, as throughout Shaughnessy Heights,
the roadside walls and hedges and the luxuriant landscaping contribute to the visual continuity.

HENRY M. LEGGAT HOUSE   **F4**
1363 The Crescent
Architect unknown, c. 1911

This attractive house recalls an eighteenth-century New England Georgian townhouse with its pedimented three-part façade, pilastered clapboard walls, hipped roof, curved entrance porch, and shuttered sash windows. This and the Macdonald house (F6) are the most American designs on The Crescent; but the flat façade characteristic of houses south of the border is here broken up by projecting bows with windows of fine curved glass.

FREDERICK M. KELLY HOUSE   **F5**
1398 The Crescent
Townley and Matheson, 1921

This low-slung house is an early example of the Dutch Colonial Revival fashion that swept Vancouver in the 1920s. The second-floor windows appear as an extended dormer in the double-sloped mansard roof. Here stucco has graduated from half-timber infill to status as a full-fledged facing material.

GEORGE E. MACDONALD HOUSE **F6**
1350 The Crescent
Architect unknown, 1914

A columnar pedimented portico introduces a Classical
Revival house that would not be out of place in nineteenth-century U.S.A. Yet the mixture of sources —
Greek Ionic capitals, Roman semicircular pediments, and
a Renaissance 'Palladian' window in the pediment —
and the silhouette-breaking dormer windows show an
indifference to accepted rules of composition in a way
that is typical of Canadian architecture. Owner George
E. Macdonald had interests in timber and mining and
was general manager of the Pacific Great Eastern Railway (now B.C. Railway). In 1922 he sold the house to
rival Alexander Robert Mann of the Canadian Northern
(now C.N.) Railway. For the past generation it has been
The Hollies guest house.

BRYCE W. FLECK HOUSE **F7**
1296 The Crescent
Probably by Honeyman and Curtis, 1929

This house for industrial supplier Fleck and the nearby
C. Carry House at 1232 The Crescent (also probably by
Honeyman and Curtis, 1929) reveal the persistence of the
Tudor mode. Stucco has taken over from wood as the
principal material. The building's attraction arises from
its detail, particularly the *porte-cochère*, stained glass,
and curved gable.

M. Y. AIVAZOFF HOUSE ('VILLA RUSSE')   **F8**
3390 The Crescent
Cleven Cox, 1921

The simpler composition and more stable horizontality of this secluded mansion are characteristic of houses of the 1920s. Italianate arches and balustrade reflect the conservative classicism of its British designer. Russian émigré Misak Y. Aivazoff opened the doors of his sumptuously furnished home to visiting Russian nobility and artists, including Grand Duke Alexander and Serge Rachmaninoff. A later occupant, B.C. Electric Company chairman Dal Grauer, added the front terrace and built a cabana in the rear (by Arthur Erickson, 1959, invisible from the street) that features a tall canopy with ten delicately linked parasols of white plastic.

L. W. SHATFORD HOUSE   **F9**
3338 The Crescent
Architect unknown, 1912

Broker and former M.L.A. Lytton W. Shatford built a particularly fine example of the Western Shingle Style. Love for wood is evident in the shingled siding and the generous ornament. Projecting rafters, heavy brackets beneath the eaves, second-storey overhang and sills, and the entrance piers all exploit the decorative use of timber.

NOEL DUMAS HOUSE ('STRATHFIELD')   **F10**
3489 Osler Street
Daniel E. White, 1972

Reportedly the largest and — at $600,000 — the most
expensive house to be built in Vancouver in two generations, this stucco and cedar mansion is the home of
Australian hotel magnate Noel Dumas. The crisp recti-
linearity is effectively broken by varied subtle projections.
Large expanses of tinted glass are recessed behind broad
overhangs and sun-screening horizontal fins. In 1973
Dumas expanded his Vancouver residential holdings by
purchasing the West Vancouver waterfront estate of
Nick Kogos (I24).

FRANK L. BUCKLEY HOUSE   **F11**
3498 Osler Street
MacKenzie and Ker, 1913

An effective and original compromise between Gothic
and Classical influences is reached in this fine house for
lumberman Buckley. The simple three-bay façade with a
central gable derives from the American Gothic cottages
of A. J. Downing, which in turn led to the typical
Ontario house of the later nineteenth century. The porch
columns and entablature, on the other hand, reflect
Roman ornament. Leaded glass windows and fine decorative woodwork reveal a high level of craftsmanship.

F. W. MORGAN HOUSE   **F12**
3538 Osler Street
R. MacKay Fripp, 1912

Stone, shingles, stucco, and timber trim are combined in this Tudor-inspired house. The right-hand gable is neatly balanced by the verandah to the left.

A. E. TULK HOUSE ('ROSEMARY')   **F13**
3689 Selkirk Street
*Maclure and Fox, 1913-15; probably completed by
Bernard Palmer at later date*

This magnificent house (costing more than $250,000) was named 'Rosemary' after lawyer and liquor magnate Tulk's only daughter. The half-timbering in which Samuel Maclure excelled is combined with white shingles and brown clapboard and an archway of brick to give the appearance of a rambling English manor. During the lengthy construction of the main building, the Tulks inhabited the small wing at the north end (by D. R. Paterson, 1912) which later became the servants' quarters and garages. The gardens were carefully laid out to compensate for the lack of view.

HUGH MCLEAN HOUSE II   F14
1264 Balfour Avenue
Probably by Townley and Matheson, 1924

This house represents a type — available in a choice of
exterior finishes — popularized in the 1920s by architects
Townley and Matheson, who may well have been the
designers here. The hipped roof drops its side eaves a
storey below the front eave, leaving a space of limited use
under the sloping roof illuminated by small circular windows. The pattern created by the combination of shapes
parallels the abstract geometry of early modernist
painting.

HUGH MCLEAN HOUSE I ('DUART')   F15
3741 Hudson Street
Grant, Henderson, and Cook, 1913

Broad asymmetrical massing, a detached central gable,
the low angular turret, and patterned shingle siding
make this house a particularly fine example of the Shingle
Style that developed in the Eastern U.S. — particularly
New England — in the 1880s. The predominantly horizontal lines contrast with the taller profile of most local
buildings, such as the adjacent Fraser house (3651
Hudson Street, 1912), now the Monastery of the
Precious Blood. Investment broker Hugh McLean built
this house then moved a block away (F14) a decade
later.

PETER THORNTON HOUSE   **F16**
1303 Matthews Avenue
Peter Thornton, 1946

Just before and after the second world war, a small group
of progressive architects, among them Peter Thornton
(of Gardiner and Thornton), created a group of houses
that abandoned traditional features. Attracted by the
International Style brought to the U.S.A. from Europe
in the 1930s, they produced the most progressive architecture in Canada. Today, houses such as this may look
dull; to contemporary Vancouverites they were startling.
Architects explained their break from tradition by claim-
ing to have discovered empirical solutions to the particular building conditions (see I31).

WILLIAM WALSH HOUSE   **F17**
3589 Granville Street
H. Murray, 1912

Fine wrought iron cresting caps the ridge of this stolid
stone and shingle home. A broad hipped roof with flaring
eaves — perhaps influenced by Samuel Maclure (see
F2) — rests on brackets. The walls are picturesquely
broken by turrets and various other projections. For the
past two decades the house, now called 'Rockland,' has
been occupied and well maintained by the John Westa-
way Society, a residential philosophical association.

DAVID DUMARESQ HOUSE   **F18**
1538 Matthews Avenue
Herbert Rudolph, 1971

The shingled double-sloped roof pierced with windows (called a mansard roof after 17th-century French architect François Mansart) is appearing on countless new and remodelled old houses. This renewed emphasis on the skyline may represent a reaction against the flat roofline of so many newer buildings. The appearance of the present house, like that of its neighbour, is mainly shingled mansard and old brick. Builder Rudolph designed both (on a subdivided large lot) as well as the J. S. Godfrey House at 3663 Alexandra Street.

WILLIAM LAMONT TAIT HOUSE   **F19**
('GLEN BRAE')
1690 Matthews Avenue
Probably by Parr and Fee, 1910

Lumber and real estate tycoon W. L. Tait built 'Glen Brae,' his 'Valley by the Mountains,' to remind him of the castles of his native Scotland. The twin domed towers make this one of the most unforgettable of Shaughnessy homes. The interior features exquisite wood finishes, stained glass windows, and an elevator. The floor of the third-storey ballroom was laid over a padding of seaweed to give it spring. The superb wrought iron fence was manufactured in Scotland. As memorable to older Vancouverites as the building itself was the day in 1925 when the Kanadian Knights of the Ku Klux Klan paraded up Granville Street into their newly purchased Tait house. 'Glen Brae' soon lost its controversial occupants, and now serves as a private hospital for the elderly.

R. S. LENNIE HOUSE **F20**
1737 Matthews Avenue
Sharp and Thompson, 1912

G. L. T. Sharp and C. J. Thompson, the original partners of a firm of architects that has dominated Vancouver architecture for more than sixty years (and
known today as Thompson, Berwick, Pratt, and Partners), began their fertile careers as traditional revivalists.
Their Georgian Revival Vancouver Club (D21), Gothic
Revival church of St. Mary's, Kerrisdale (West 37th
Avenue at Larch Street, 1913), and the present large
Tudor Revival house for lawyer Lennie display the range
of styles available to better trained architects.

ROBERT E. VEITH HOUSE **F21**
3850 Marguerite Street
Architect unknown, 1914

The classical formality of this shuttered clapboard house
reflects the Georgian architecture of the Eastern U.S.A.
Even the somewhat top-heavy pedimented portico, the
door with fan- and side-lights, and the roof dormers are
true to their source. The Georgian style reached Southern
Ontario around 1800, so the house of singer and dry-
cleaner Veith might be interpreted as part of a Canadian
architectural revival.

GEORGE WALKEM HOUSE **F22**
3990 Marguerite Street
R. Mackay Fripp, 1913-14

This twin-gabled house finished in roughcast derives from the later 19th-century suburban 'bungalow' of the English middle class. The bungalow — a term meaning Bengalese — originated in the British colonial house in India. Architect Fripp may have encountered the manner in his native Britain or during his residence in Australia and New Zealand. The large leaded central window, end buttresses, and bracketed eaves of businessman Walkem's house deviate from the English Colonial Bungalow mode and show the continuing influence on Vancouver of the Tudor and Gothic Revivals. A better known derivative of this manner was the pervasive California Bungalow (see H8 and H44).

B. T. LEA HOUSE **F23**
4051 Marguerite Street
John A. Pauw, 1930

The continuous horizontal lines and broad overhanging roofs of this angled corner house reveal the influence of the great American architect Frank Lloyd Wright. Other Wrightian features are the many doors linking inside with out and the elimination of the basement. Transient Dutch architect Pauw offered a pleasing contrast of materials with the variegated brick ground floor, wood upper storey, and shingle roof.

A. B. WEEKS HOUSE **F24**
1808 West King Edward Avenue
Architect unknown, 1923

Spanish explorers reached this area shortly before the
Royal Navy's Captain Vancouver, but Spaniards never
settled on the British Columbia mainland. Architectural
revivalists, however, have been indifferent to such historical details. The Mission Style, developed in the once
Spanish-ruled American Southwest, found fertile breed-
ing grounds in Vancouver. This white stucco house
recalls early California missions with its low profile and
repetitive shaped gables; it lacks only the customary red
tiled roof. This south side of King Edward Avenue marks
the beginning of the second Shaughnessy subdivision,
dignified but with houses smaller than those in the first.

JOHN HENDRY HOUSE **F25**
3802 Angus Drive
Probably by Maclure and Fox, c. 1912-15

Lumber magnate John Hendry, a native of New Bruns-
wick who came to B.C. in 1873 to work at the Moodyville
Sawmill (see I7) and became president of B.C. Mills,
Timber and Trading Company (B27), abandoned his
large West End mansion at Burnaby and Jervis Streets
(1903; demolished in 1968 and remembered in the name
of the Hendry House apartments) for this enormous
Shaughnessy home. The Tudor Revival style is repeated
at the other end of the triple lot by the coach house, now
converted into a private home and painted in different
colours. The Hendry house competes in size with Judge
Aulay MacAulay Morrison's house across the street
(1789 Matthews Avenue, by Maclure and Fox, 1912).

W. F. HUNTTING HOUSE   **F26**
3689 Angus Drive
Maclure and Fox, 1911

The horizontally proportioned roughcast façade termi-
nated at each end by a cross-gable and topped by a steep
roof resembles houses by English architect C. F. A.
Voysey, teacher of Cecil Croker Fox. Architect Fox was
the same age and belonged to the same clubs as American-
born lumberman W. Foster Huntting. Here Fox's own
artistic personality is seen emerging from beneath the
Tudor shadow of his senior Victoria partner, Samuel
Maclure.

W. F. SALSBURY HOUSE   **F27**
1790 Angus Drive
A. A. Cox, 1912

The white roughcast walls, prominent shaped gables,
and deep balcony link this unusual house to the Mission
Style (see F24). The picturesque massing and broad
roofs, however, betray the dominant influence of old
English buildings upon English-born architect Cox.
William Ferriman Salsbury, who arrived in B.C. on the
first transcontinental train, was one of the many C.P.R.
officials who settled in the railway's Shaughnessy Heights
development.

ANGUS PLACE **F28**
1660 Angus Drive; 3610-30 Alexandra Street
Tanner/Kay, 1973

A large house was demolished and its lot subdivided to allow the construction of this introverted 'four-house village.' The luxurious homes face away from the street towards a communal pool and sauna. Their design consciously combines modern and traditional elements; clean walls and shed roofs admit such features as whimsical arches and panelled doors with fanlights. The mature plantings and high wall along the perimeter have been preserved.

JAMES MCGAVIN HOUSE **F29**
1652 Marpole Avenue
Architect unknown, 1940

Bakery owner McGavin built this long and low house in a period of architectural uncertainty. Modernist tendencies which had emerged in the 30s were balanced by the traditional nature of Shaughnessy Heights. The result is a dormer-pierced mansard roof — a form that has recently become quite fashionable (see F18) — and a curved central gable with eighteenth-century French overtones. The house is one of a number sharing the enormous lot originally covered only by the Tudor home of C.P.R. official Richard Marpole (1615 Angus Drive, probably by J. J. Honeyman, 1909); the present street and a district of South Vancouver (see H23) were named after Marpole.

ARTHUR BRENCHLEY HOUSE **F30**
3351 Granville Street
Maclure and Fox, 1912

This home for wholesale grocer Arthur Brenchley is the best Vancouver representative of the kind of middle-sized Tudor Revival house for which Samuel Maclure became famous in Victoria. Half-timbering is reduced to vertical strips of dark wood alternating with stucco rectangles on the upper storey and beneath the central gable. The entrance off the *porte-cochère* at the rear leads to a fine galleried staircase hall typical of houses by Maclure and Fox. A well-preserved Maclure and Fox interior accessible to the public is that of Cecil Green Park (6251 N.W. Marine Drive) on the U.B.C. Campus, built in 1911-12 for lawyer E. P. Davis.

Driving Tour   G

False Creek

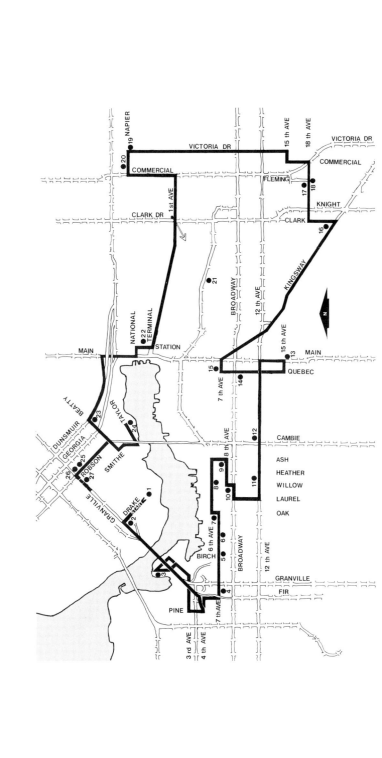

FALSE CREEK

To the south of Vancouver's downtown peninsula lies
False Creek, a tidal inlet that was once much more of a
waterway than it is today. It stretched some three and
one-half crooked miles eastward from English Bay as far
as today's Clark Drive. At high tide it joined Burrard
Inlet at the present Columbia Street in Chinatown.

In 1887, the C.P.R. built its yards along the north
shore (G1) and a railway trestle (soon to be demolished)
spanned it to Kitsilano. Fearing that the trestle might
interfere with marine traffic, the federal government
placed the creek under the Navigable Waters Protection
Act. Ironically this act was to be used to the detriment
of False Creek.

The Great Northern Railway followed the C.P.R. onto
False Creek and erected its terminus on filled land adjacent to Pender Street (B7). A decade later, the Great
Northern and the Canadian Northern Pacific acquired
terminal rights to the eastern end of False Creek (G22),
and one-third of the waterway was filled in to provide
land for yards and a station. Main Street, which since
1871 had bridged the creek a mile from its eastern end
to link Vancouver with the road to New Westminster
(now Kingsway), was now on solid ground.

The railways were followed by heavy industry. Vancouver became — and remains — the centre of the
mammoth B.C. forest industry. Sawmills needed water
and train tracks, and False Creek offered both. To increase the available industrial sites, the city acquired
rights to the creek bed and 'reclaimed' hundreds of acres
of land. Water became a negative resource. The federal
government entered the scene in 1915 by conducting
massive land fill and creating Granville Island (G3),
using the Navigable Waters Protection Act as its legal
springboard.

Smoke-belching factories and mills lined the creek, and
log booms occupied what remained of the waterway.
Land fill continues; in 1972 the city began to fill the
area west of Main Street to build the high-speed
Columbia-Quebec Connector roadway (work was halted
in mid-1973). False Creek has shrunk to about one-
quarter of its original 1,000 acres.

In the late 1960s the city finally decided that something had to be done with False Creek. Many industrial
plants had relocated, and the unsightliness of those remaining and the deterioration of the residential area was
finally recognized. In 1971 the False Creek Study Group,

composed of private consultants and city officials, began to investigate redevelopment possibilities for the land around the Creek, most of which is owned by the three levels of government and the C.P.R.'s Marathon Realty. City council has established a special committee on False Creek. Present development guidelines envisage housing for 20-30,000 people of various incomes mixed with commercial areas, marinas, and parkland. In November 1973 city planners recommended that only 25 per cent of the housing be for families with children. Redevelopment officially began in 1973 with the demolition of several industrial buildings and the opening of a small park near the foot of Oak Street (see G7). Detailed proposals and designs will follow shortly.

Once Vancouver's outskirts, False Creek now occupies the heart of the city. Its future, like its water, is still cloudy. Its past and present are still very visible, and these form the subject of the present tour.

Distance: 15 miles.
Time: 2-2½ hours.

C.P.R. SHOPS   **G1**
East end of Drake Street
Various architects, begun 1886

The C.P.R. originally intended to develop its shops and
yards on the south side of False Creek because of the
superior water supply there. But Vancouver's nervous
merchants feared that a rival town might be established.
They convinced city council to offer the railway a
twenty-year exemption from taxes in return for locating
on the north shore of the Creek. The railway agreed,
and in 1886 began to bring its machinery here from the
former shops at Yale in the Fraser Canyon. A group of
1- and 2-storey brick and timber buildings, simple
industrial structures with no pretence to 'style,' fill the
complex. The tallest is the brick stores office (c. 1910).
The oldest are closer to the water, out of sight from
Drake Street: the shiplap coachyard office, reportedly a
depot moved here from elsewhere, the board-and-batten
former cross-arm shed, and the former oil house probably
all date from the 1880s. The old roundhouse stands at
the north end of the complex. The yards are once again
relocating, this time to nearby Coquitlam. This prime
land on the north shore of False Creek will soon be
redeveloped by Canadian Pacific's Marathon Realty as
part of the False Creek project. Present plans call for the
complete demolition of the old structures.

Most of the men employed in the C.P.R. shops and
roundhouse built homes near this end of Granville Street.
The workers' community became known as Yaletown,
after Yale. The first houses to be erected here were
brought to Vancouver from Yale in the mid-1880s by
flatcar. The houses and nearby Yaletown Church (see
H47) have disappeared.

YALE HOTEL   **G2**
1300 Granville Street
Architect unknown, 1890

Located some distance from the developed — and policed
— part of Vancouver, Yaletown became notorious for its
night life. The Yale Hotel (originally called the Colonial
Hotel) was a centre of this activity. Its decorative brickwork, mansard roof, and arched windows contrast with
the bland buildings that later grew up around it.

NATIONAL MACHINERY COMPANY LIMITED   **G3**
Duranleau Street, Granville Island
Architects unknown, begun 1920

The federal government created 34½-acre Granville
Island in 1915 with mud dredged from False Creek.
About fifty industrial plants were erected. Train cars,
heavy equipment, trucks, and automobiles share the
narrow roadways in the shadow of the Granville Bridge
(the third bridge here, opened in 1954). Many of the
factories, like this plant for manufacturing heavy equipment, are built of galvanized iron. The large basilica-like
structure is not unlike rural barns with the tall central
'nave' and lower 'aisles.' Heavy industry will probably
soon vacate the island, and there are plans for residential
and recreational development. A portent of things to
come is the Creekhouse, a former factory on Johnston
Street renovated in 1973 to become a restaurant and
offices.

SEYMOUR MEDICAL CLINIC   **G4**
1530 West 7th Avenue
Rhone and Iredale, 1969

Exciting new architecture provides an attractive and
highly functional setting for two dozen physicians. Above
the recessed ground floor reception and pharmacy are
five 'clusters,' each with its separate waiting area, nurses'
station, examining rooms, and consulting offices. Each
cluster is sufficiently small to give the intimate feeling of
a doctor's office. Planted light courts further break up
the space. Poured concrete, the basic structural material,
is used inside for columns, textured walls, and an effective honeycomb ceiling.

WILLIAM HUNT HOUSE   **G5**
2300 Birch Street
Architect unknown, 1910

The Fairview area, situated on the hillside south of
False Creek between Granville and Cambie Streets, developed rapidly in the years after 1900. Fairview's developers succeeded in attracting a number of well-to-do
residents such as engineer William Hunt. His house has
a granite-faced ground floor, a wide verandah, and a
corner tower, all features popular among larger Vancouver houses. Fairview never succeeded as a high-class
development because of competition from Shaughnessy
Heights — and an odorous sewer outfall that then existed
at the bottom of the hill.

1148-1164 WEST 7TH AVENUE G6
Samuel McLeod, 1911-13

These four houses built by speculator McLeod comprised part of a seven-unit development for middle-class occupants. *Province* publisher Walter C. Nichol used to live on the site; his removal to Shaughnessy Heights (F2) and the demolition of his mansion typify Fairview's failure as an expensive residential area. Architect Neil Pelman rehabilitated these houses in 1972 in an attempt to instil new life into the decaying district. Pelman's fine design makes no attempt at an accurate restoration; comparison with Nos. 1130-1140 shows that he chose to add upper balconies and adopt handsome new colour schemes.

1017 WEST 7TH AVENUE G7
Architect unknown, 1914

Housva Takehara built this tenement for Japanese labourers employed in nearby sawmills. Two breaks in massing and a stepped balcony help the house cling to the steep Fairview hillside. Only 18 feet wide, the building stretches 110 feet to the rear of the property and makes maximum use of a 25-foot lot. Its floor space ratio is similar to that of a West End high-rise. Asian workers continued to inhabit the building until the removal of 23,000 coastal Japanese to interior towns and Prairie farms during the second world war. The building has recently been modified to accommodate nine rental suites.

The new False Creek Public Area is accessible from the foot of Oak Street, one block below this house. The city's temporary information office is located at 1101 West 6th Avenue.

ALBERTA LUMBER COMPANY LIMITED   **G8**
790 West 6th Avenue
Architect unknown, 1912

This classically proportioned 2-storey frame building, well preserved inside and out, provides retail and office space for Alberta Lumber. The company used to operate one of the dozen or so sawmills located on False Creek between the Granville and the Cambie Street Bridges. The large mill occupied the reclaimed ground opposite the store, now used for heavy equipment storage. A few hundred yards past the timber storage sheds at the water's edge one obtains a good view of False Creek and the log booms being stored by Bay Forest Products Limited, the last operative sawmill on False Creek (G24).

B.C. TELEPHONE COMPANY   **G9**
COMPUTER CENTRE
West 7th Avenue at Ash Street
Erickson/Massey, 1969-70

This attractive fortress-like structure designed by Gary Hanson houses the telephone company's computers. It was intended for a private data processing firm, but the business did not survive long enough to take possession. The sense of impenetrability is reinforced by the raw concrete walls and the noisy ventilation fans by the entrance. The building can support four additional storeys; they may either continue the inward slope of the mezzanine or else angle back towards the street and zigzag upwards.

805 BROADWAY CENTRE   **G10**
805 West Broadway
Vladimir Plavsic and Associates, 1972-73

Many tall new buildings have adopted distinctive shapes
to achieve liveliness and individuality. This textured
concrete structure has a steep pointed roof that is recognizable for miles around. Behind the building the wall
angles down the steep hillside. This is one of a number
of medical-dental office buildings recently erected in this
area adjacent to the Vancouver General Hospital (G11).

VANCOUVER GENERAL HOSPITAL: **G11**
THE HEALTH CENTRE FOR CHILDREN
West 12th Avenue near Heather Street
Townley and Matheson, 1944

The Health Centre for Children is a fine example of
'proto-modern' public architecture, more dressed up than
industrial buildings of the same era (compare H2).
Horizontal bands along and between the windows,
columnar shafts behind the entrance, and the curved
staircase 'railings' typify the streamlined ornament inspired by the machine aesthetic. The hospital has grown
from the small City Hospital at Beatty and Pender
Streets (1886) to one of the largest in the world. Parts
of the original Fairview Building (by Grant and Henderson, 1903-05) survive behind this block as a portion of
the Heather Pavilion. The largest structure in the hospital complex is the Centennial Pavilion (by Townley,
Matheson, and Partners, 1956-58), whose four wings
radiate from a central service core.

CITY HALL   **G12**
453 West 12th Avenue
Townley and Matheson, 1935-36

After a decade of bickering, the present city hall site was
chosen in 1935 with prodding from Mayor G. G.
McGeer, who wanted to cement links with newly annexed
South Vancouver. A special bond issue helped finance
the million-dollar structure during economic hard times.
The hard-edged classicism of the austere white walls and
column-like shafts appears in government buildings of
the 1930s from Munich to Moscow. Modernistic geometric ornament is found on the green spandrels between
the windows and a frieze above each block. A 4-storey
annex was built to the north in 1968-70 (by Townley,
Matheson, and Partners).

POSTAL STATION C   **G13**
Main Street and 15th Avenue
A. Campbell Hope, 1914-15

Banded stone ground floor, coupled pilasters, steep roofs,
and a picturesque clock tower combine to create Vancouver's best example of Beaux-arts Classicism. Carved
Haddington Island stone contrasts effectively with the
brick walls of the upper floors. The design may be seen
as a flattened reprise of the Main Post Office downtown
(C10). The building was apparently intended to dominate its characterless low commercial neighbours, for the
upper storey originally had no use. Since the Post Office's
departure to a new building nearby (see G14), the
structure has been occupied by several federal government departments. It is currently used by the R.C.M.P.

EVANGELISTIC TABERNACLE   **G14**

N.W. Corner East 10th Avenue and Quebec Street

Parr and Fee, 1909-10

Originally the Mount Pleasant Presbyterian Church, this building combines Romanesque Revival round entrance arches and corner turret (now sheathed in shiny sheet metal) with Late Gothic depressed pointed arches. The whole is tidily held together with brickwork trimmed in stone. This intersection is the heart of old Mount Pleasant, the high ground at the end of the Main Street bridge that was the first district to be developed south of False Creek. The Mount Pleasant Baptist Church (by Burke, Horwood, and White, 1909-10) adopts the Tudor Revival half-timber-and-stone combination frequently found in private houses. The Holy Trinity Ukranian Greek Orthodox Church (1948) has the traditional bulbous 'onion' domes above an otherwise bland stucco building. The Harry Stevens Building (by Gerald Hamilton and Associates, 1963), contains federal government offices and the new Postal Station C (see G13).

QUEBEC MANOR   **G15**
101 East 7th Avenue
Townsend and Townsend, 1912

Two immodest female figures energetically support the
heavy pediment that forms the frontispiece to this mar-
vellous 4-storey apartment building. Originally the Mt.
Stephen Apartments, it also features patterned yellow
and red brickwork, bay windows, and curved festooned
wrought iron balconies.

The tour proceeds along Kingsway, the untidy
thoroughfare (once known as Westminster Road) that
follows the trail begun between New Westminster and
Vancouver in 1861. It was paralleled in 1891 by the
interurban tram line through Burnaby's Central Park
(along the route of today's Vanness Avenue). A glance
at the map suggests that planners had difficulty reconcil-
ing oblique Kingsway with the gridiron street pattern.

PARAPLEGIC LODGE   **G16**
3655 Clark Drive
Downs/Archambault, 1972

This handsome complex is a transitional residence for
paraplegics who have left rehabilitation centres and are
preparing themselves for a return to work and to the
community. Three units, broken into small-scaled portions by the disconnected sloping roofs, surround an inner
courtyard onto which opens a common lounge and dining room. Supergraphics on the cedar siding identify the
units. The plan offers residents relative privacy while still
enabling them to oversee each other's activities should
the need for assistance arise.

ST. MARK'S LUTHERAN CHURCH   **G17**
1553 East 18th Avenue
Architect unknown, probably 1911

Originally the Robson Memorial Methodist Church, this
strikingly handsome shingle and half-timber church was
built to serve the Cedar Cottage district. Named after a
farm building in the area, Cedar Cottage was a stop on
the interurban tram from Vancouver to New Westminster. Moses Gibson had a 19-acre ranch here in the
1890s; two decades later the hill and nearby Trout Lake
(now in John Hendry Park, passed next on the tour)
attracted well-to-do homeowners. The fine houses of
Cedar Cottage are now mostly gone (see G18), and the
church alone reflects the elegance of a past era.

3412-3436 FLEMING STREET;   **G18**
1604 EAST 18TH AVENUE
P. & H. Builders Limited, 1972-73

Five simple houses represent the typical single-family
dwelling erected by builders in Vancouver and its
suburbs today. A large proportion of the restricted space
is occupied by the ground-level 2-car carports. Four are
stuccoed with wood trim and the fifth faced entirely in
wood. These five houses are crowded onto the site of the
home built in 1911 for factory owner Alfred P. Stewart
(demolished 1972), one of the many finer houses that
graced this district.

W. H. COPP HOUSE   **G19**
1110 Victoria Drive
J. P. Malluson, 1910-11

Realtor W. H. Copp spared little expense in building his
fine home. A domed corner turret, columnar portico, and
impressive stained and bevelled glass windows lend
elegance, while the stone wall and generous landscaping
offer seclusion. Numerous larger houses were erected in
this Grandview area as it developed around 1910. The
Grandview Hospital across the street (1090 Victoria
Drive) was built at the same time.

ROBERTSON PRESBYTERIAN CHURCH   **G20**
1795 Napier Street
*B.C. Mills, Timber and Trading Company, 1908;
addition 1921*

A group of Presbyterians erected a prefabricated hall
here in newly cleared Grandview as their church building. The vertical strips that cover the bolted panels are
characteristic of the B.C. Mills system (see B27). The
south wing on Napier Street is a later addition. The
handsome turreted shingled house across the street (1036
Salsbury, now Glen Hospital) was built in 1908 by John
J. Miller, an Australian realtor and auctioneer who
came to Vancouver in 1903 and became a city alderman
and the first president of the Vancouver Exhibition
Association (now the Pacific National Exhibition; see
I6).

The next portion of the tour passes through the retail
centre of Vancouver's Italian community. The best restaurants and shops are located on Commercial Drive just
south of 1st Avenue.

THE THIRTY-NINE STEPS **G21**
770 Great Northern Way
(seen from 1335 East 1st Avenue)
Robert Rapske, 1971-72

Beyond the flats in the distance to the left is the Thirty-Nine Steps, a tiered apartment building that climbs up the hillside somewhat like the hill towns of owner-builder John Zen's native Italy. The number of steps in the statue-lined staircase beside it almost coincided with those in John Buchan's famous novel (actually there are only thirty-eight); hence the name. The 131 suites look out on the industrial flats that were once covered by False Creek. The First Avenue Viaduct crosses the track-covered lowland and leads to Terminal Avenue with its many distribution warehouses. Other streets in the area bear such imaginative names as Industrial, Northern, Central, Southern, Western, and Station.

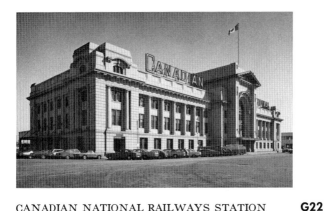

CANADIAN NATIONAL RAILWAYS STATION **G22**
1150 Station Street
Pratt and Ross, perhaps with John Schofield, 1917-19

The Canadian Northern Pacific Railway, the second
transcontinental railroad and now a part of the nationally
owned C.N.R., obtained terminal rights on False Creek
in return for extensive pledges to the city that included
the erection of a large downtown hotel (realized in the
Hotel Vancouver, D2). The station and the yards to the
east are on filled land. This part of Main Street was a
bridge. The Great Northern Railway station (by Fred
Townley, 1915-17; see B7) just to the north was
demolished in 1965 to save taxes. Its site remains a parking lot. The two railways (the Great Northern is now
called the Burlington Northern) have since shared the
present facilities. The station adopts the Neoclassical
Revival mode, mandatory in those years for a metropoli-
tan terminus; here a central arch is flanked by colon-
naded wings.

BEATTY STREET DRILL HALL **G23**
620 Beatty Street
Department of Public Works, 1899-1901

Drill halls and armouries were traditionally rendered in
a medieval mode because of the association between the
army and old forts. Two round turrets and a crenellated
parapet give this military drill hall the appearance of a
fortress as does the rusticated stone trim. The building
guards the western entrance to the Georgia Viaduct (by
Phillips, Barratt, Hillier, Jones, and Partners, 1969-72),
a six-lane divided highway over the C.P.R. yards. It was
approved by the city before the decision to reject downtown expressways, but nevertheless executed as planned.

BAY FOREST PRODUCTS LIMITED **G24**
730 Taylor Street
Architect and date unknown

Bay Forest Products operates the last sawmill to remain
on False Creek. A wooden shed along the roadway
protects the 'green chain,' the conveyor that carries
sawn lumber to sorters. Beyond the shed rise the wood-
and metal-clad walls of the sawmill proper. Lumber is
piled here and on yards by the other side of the Connaught (Cambie Street) Bridge, parts of which were
completed before 1890.

THE ORILLIA   **G25**
611 Robson Street
Parr and Fee, 1903

A downtown anomaly, this frame rooming house sits a
scant block from the Granville and Georgia intersection.
The building — a kind of early apartment house — was
built by industrialist W. L. Tait (see F19 and D35) and
contained six residential units. It appears to be a trio of
joined houses, each with its sheltered portico. The open
balcony provides communication between the three
sections. The ground floor was altered for commercial
purposes in 1907 as the business district moved west; the
Orillia Pool Room was its first commercial tenant.

ROYAL BANK OF CANADA   **G26**
798 Granville Street
Underwood, McKinley, Cameron, and Associates, 1962-63

A handsome façade of aluminum, granite, and glass
covers a branch bank and four floors of rental offices.
Because of the narrow site, the bank occupies two levels
joined by an escalator. A fountain (by Lionel A. J.
Thomas) was inserted at the corner to enliven what
might otherwise have been a dead spot after banking
hours. Pedestrian activity along Granville Street is
encouraged further by the conversion of this stretch into
an automobile-free mall.

ORPHEUM THEATRE   **G27**
884 Granville Street
B. M. Priteca, 1926-27; F. J. Peters, associated architect

This lavish western outpost of vaudeville's Chicago-based
Orpheum Circuit was the largest theatre in Canada and
the Pacific Northwest. Theatre specialist B. Marcus
Priteca of Seattle created the multi-levelled foyer and
2,870-seat auditorium. The marble and travertine walls
with their profuse Spanish arches, cast stone ornament,
and rich plaster ceilings competed with the most luxurious theatres on the continent. The Orpheum presents a
narrow stone entrance façade to Granville Street's
Theatre Row and a 25-foot-wide concourse leads over
the alley to the auditorium, situated on less expensive land
on Seymour Street. In 1973 the owner, Famous Players
Theatres, announced its intention of subdividing the
Orpheum into several smaller cinemas. The city responded by committing itself to buy the theatre, restore
it, and make it the new home of the Vancouver Sym-
phony Orchestra (now resident in the Queen Elizabeth
Theatre, C34).

Point Grey
and South Vancouver

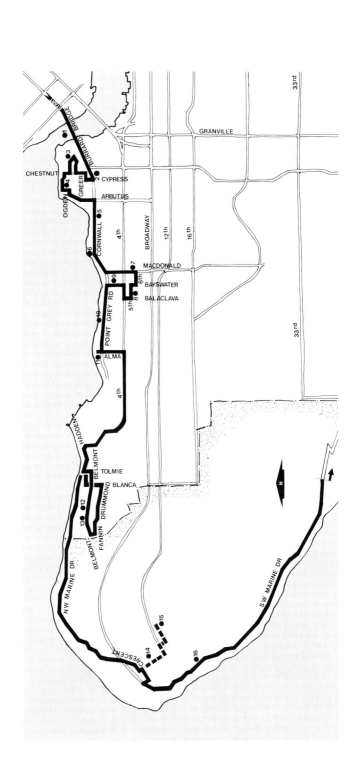

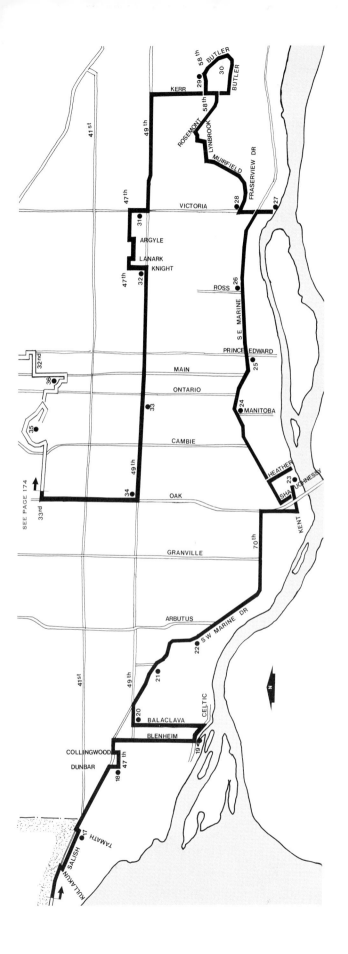

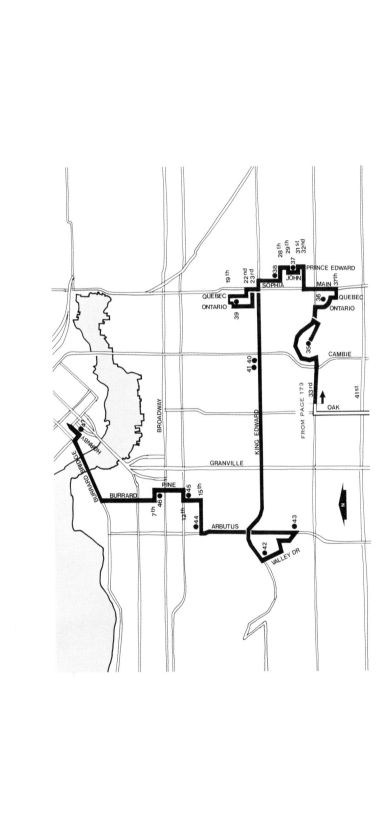

19 th
22 nd
23 rd
28 th
29 th
31 st
32 nd
●38
37
JOHN
PRINCE EDWARD
QUEBEC
SOPHIA
MAIN
37th
QUEBEC
●36
ONTARIO
●39
ONTARIO
●35
CAMBIE
41 40
●
FROM PAGE 173
33 rd
41st
OAK
KING EDWARD
BROADWAY
GRANVILLE
N
PINE
●45
46
15 th
BURRARD
7 th
BURRARD BRIDGE
HORNBY
47
12th
●44
ARBUTUS
●43
42
VALLEY DR

POINT GREY AND SOUTH VANCOUVER

A glance at the map reveals that the downtown peninsula in which the first five walking tours were concentrated constitutes only a small portion of the City of
Vancouver. It forms a tiny offshoot of the larger peninsula that terminates to the west in Point Grey. Indians
have inhabited the area for millenia. The first Europeans
to sight the sandy cliffs of Point Grey were the crew of
Commander Narváez, who investigated the Strait (or
Gulf) of Georgia for Spain in 1791. In June of the
following year, Britain's Captain George Vancouver
reached the area and explored it more carefully; he
named the point after his friend, naval Captain George
Grey. Vancouver exchanged civilities with the Spanish
commanders Galiano and Valdéz on the shores of the
peninsula, and the name Spanish Banks commemorates
their rendezvous.

Europeans showed no further interest in the peninsula
for two-thirds of a century. In 1859 surveyor Walter
Moberly, employed by the New Westminster-based Royal
Engineers, reserved land at the end of Point Grey and at
Jericho on English Bay for naval and military purposes.

About the same time, farmers began to settle in the
fertile lowlands at the mouth of the North Arm of the
Fraser River. The first homesteaders were the Irish
brothers Samuel and Fitzgerald McCleery, who pre-
empted district lots 315 and 316 on the south slope of the
city in 1862. Their first substantial farmhouse, built near
the foot of today's Macdonald Street in 1873, was probably the first permanent residence within the present
boundaries of Vancouver. It was demolished in 1956 by
the park board as part of clearing operations for a public
golf course (see also H21). The McCleerys were soon
followed by the Magees, Moles, Shannons, and others,
and a farm community developed around the McCleery's
home (see H21). The loosely defined settlement on both
sides of the river became known as North Arm; in 1894
the name of the post office was changed to Eburne (after
Sea Island settler W. H. Eburne), and in 1916 the mainland part was renamed Marpole (after C.P.R. official
Richard Marpole; see F29).

While the southern edge of the peninsula developed
quietly, the northern part became earmarked for urban
expansion. Land as far south as today's 16th Avenue was
incorporated into Vancouver in 1886. Most of the area
from Trafalgar Street on the west to Ontario Street on
the east, and from False Creek to about 53rd Avenue

became part of the immense district lot 526 acquired by the C.P.R. Urban pressures necessitated incorporation, and in 1892 the land from 16th Avenue south to the Fraser River, from today's Boundary Road westward to the Strait of Georgia, was organized as the District of South Vancouver.

From the start South Vancouver was settled by two distinct social groups. The eastern part was made up primarily of members of the working class who had spread from Strathcona and the East End, mostly British born although there were also members of the ethnic minorities. The western part was populated mainly by the professional and managerial classes, many born in Eastern Canada, who had migrated from the West End. Social tensions and conflicting attitudes towards development led the portion west of Cambie Street to separate from South Vancouver in 1906; two years later it was incorporated as the Municipality of Point Grey.

Point Grey's already healthy tax base was given a boost by the development within its borders of Shaughnessy Heights. Citizens consistently voted municipal improvements. As a result the area has streets with planted boulevard strips and numerous parks. In 1922 Point Grey enacted the first zoning by-law in Canada with controls that clearly differentiated between residential and commercial areas.

The principal shopping district became Kerrisdale just north of the McCleerys' farm. Stores developed along 41st Avenue where it is crossed by the tracks that were laid in 1902 to the canneries at Steveston. Local resident Mrs. William MacKinnon was invited to name the line's 41st Avenue stop; she called it Kerrisdale after her family home in Scotland and unknowingly gave the name to the larger area.

South Vancouver, in contrast to Point Grey, became a working class suburb whose low-income homeowners voted for low taxes and few services. The area was never properly surveyed and has no integrated plan. Streets are narrow and poorly aligned; residential areas often contain commercial and industrial uses, and few parks were deliberately planned.

Point Grey and South Vancouver were reunited when both amalgamated with the City of Vancouver in 1927. Despite the supposed equalization of services, the physical and economic nature of the original divisions remain. To a substantial degree Cambie Street still forms a boundary line between the middle and working classes.

Vancouver is almost fully settled. Champlain Heights in the southeast sector (H29-30) is the last portion to be developed, unless one considers the 100-acre military lands at Jericho (originally called Jerry's Cove after logger Jeremiah Rogers) turned over to the city in 1973. The tip of Point Grey, containing the University of British Columbia (H14-16) and the forested University Endowment Lands, lies outside Vancouver's jurisdiction. The future of the Endowment Lands is uncertain; they may be left green, used for university expansion, or, as now seems likely, designated for residential development.

Since the city has reached its capacity for single-family dwellings, popular pressures are leading towards denser development. Kitsilano is rapidly becoming converted to 3-storey multiple-dwellings (H43); Kerrisdale has a high-rise apartment district, and other areas are undergoing physical change.

The driving tour of this area is long, and motorists may wish to divide it into two segments. One may easily return downtown after visiting H22; in this way, the constituent areas of Point Grey and South Vancouver will be seen with their separate identities intact.

Distance: 45 miles
Time: 3½-4 hours

BURRARD STREET BRIDGE   **H1**

J. R. Grant, engineer, 1930-32; Sharp and Thompson, consulting architects

Large-scale development in Point Grey and South Vancouver during the 1920s rendered the old Granville Street Bridge inadequate. In 1927 city council commissioned Major J. R. Grant to design a two-level bridge at Burrard Street for cars and trains. The Public Art Commission and other civic groups forced the building of a single-decked bridge and insisted upon architectural collaboration. Grant's steel structure was camouflaged by Sharp and Thompson's massive concrete pylons with modernistic marine ornament. A civic centre was planned for the north end, but the city hall was relocated on Cambie Street (G12) instead.

COCA-COLA BOTTLING PLANT   **H2**
1818 Cornwall Avenue
Mathers and Haldenby, 1942

Unadorned orange brick and broad windows that expose the bottling operation seem to be tightly wrapped around a reinforced concrete frame. The austere planar lines make the building a fine early Canadian venture into the mature International Style. The square entrance arch and the tall 4-storey water filtration tower break up the simple geometry into an abstract pattern. The flashing rooftop billboard is a jarring later addition.

CENTENNIAL MUSEUM AND   H3
H. R. MACMILLAN PLANETARIUM
1100 Chestnut Street
Gerald Hamilton and Associates, 1967-68

A distinctive conical dome, associated by some with a flying saucer and by others with an inverted tea cup, crowns the attractive planetarium donated to the city by H. R. MacMillan. The planetarium was a strikingly different last-minute addition inserted among the Centennial Museum's three formal exhibition galleries with their delicate lacework walls of white precast concrete. The stilted dome has become a Vancouver landmark, indeed perhaps the only architectural form with which Vancouver citizens have identified. Sculptor George Norris's popular Crab guards the entrance to the buildings. These structures and their semi-underground neighbour, the Major Matthews Building (by McCarter, Nairne, and Partners, 1971-72) occupied by the City Archives, comprise the nucleus of a new cultural centre on Kitsilano Point. Now called Vanier Park, the area is a former Indian reserve augmented by landfill. The complex began with the nearby Maritime Museum (by Raymond O. Harrison and C. B. K. Van Norman and Associates, 1958). Beside the latter rests the 80-ton R.C.M.P. Arctic patrol vessel *St. Roch* (built in 1928 at Burrard Dry Dock, I8) that twice conquered the Northwest Passage. Its 66-foot-high shingle and glass A-frame shelter was built in 1966 and was also designed by Harrison and Van Norman.

An admission fee is charged to visit the museum collections and the planetarium.

K. G. TERRISS HOUSE — H4
1970 Ogden Avenue
K. G. Terriss, 1971

Cedar shingles and glass, materials favoured by many local architects, cover this exuberantly imaginative house strategically set on Kitsilano Point. The angle of the plan exploits the spectacular mountain views and allows too a peek at the large monkey tree (imported from Chile in large numbers before the opening of the Panama Canal in 1914) on the adjacent lawn. Despite the house's explicit modernity, it respects the size and scale of its older neighbours. Parkland across the street joins the Planetarium complex with Kitsilano Park and Beach, whose central feature is C.P.R. engine No. 374 that led the first train into Vancouver.

IMPERIAL OIL SERVICE STATION — H5
2210 Cornwall Avenue
Probably by Imperial Oil Engineering Department, 1932

Gasoline stations have always sought to remain abreast of the most fashionable architectural styles. In the 1930s the Spanish Colonial Revival was one such popular mode; its white stucco walls, arched doorways, and red tile roofs give this structure its charm. During the 1950s and 1960s most service stations adopted the cool and precise geometry of the International Style. Most have recently been refaced with warmer materials such as rough stone (Texaco), old brick (Chevron), and red cedar (Shell), each particular company finding its own stylistic trademark. This station has probably escaped renovation because of its restricted site rather than in appreciation of its design.

LOVICK P. BROWN HOUSE   **H6**
2615 Point Grey Road
C. B. K. Van Norman, 1938

Charles Van Norman, a native of Ontario trained at the University of Manitoba, designed a number of influential houses in the 1930s that paved the way for Vancouver's modernism of the following decade. This home for metallurgist L. P. Brown, called a Cape Cod Cottage in its time, was inspired by the domestic architecture of the American colonies. Like earlier houses in related manners (compare F4, F21), the building has bevelled clapboard siding, shuttered windows, and a sloped roof. What is innovative is the reduction of forms to bare essentials. From here it was a short and logical step to the radically non-historical creations of such architects as Peter Thornton (I22), R. A. D. Berwick (I30), C. E. Pratt (I31), and Van Norman himself.

2100-BLOCK MACDONALD STREET   **H7**
Architects unknown, begun 1912

The Kitsilano district, named after Chief Khahtsahlano whose village near Prospect Point was appropriated for Stanley Park, developed rapidly in the years after 1909 with the completion of the second Granville Street Bridge and streetcar lines along Fourth Avenue and Broadway. It became popular as a less expensive alternative to the West End. Endless rows of developer-built houses set back uniformly from the street soon lined the gridiron streets. Many, like the present group, resemble the typical West End houses of the preceding few years (compare E8).

2900-3000 BLOCKS WEST 5TH AVENUE   **H8**
Architects unknown, begun 1912

The favourite house type of Vancouver builders in the
years 1910-25 was the 'California Bungalow.' These
inexpensive homes spread throughout the western U.S.A.
and Canada by means of pattern books advertising stock
plans that could be purchased for a few dollars. The
typical California Bungalow is an informal single-storey
house (frequently having an understated second floor)
with a verandah, one or more gables facing the street,
and loving use of wood detail — often with cobblestone
or (as here) rough 'clinker brick' chimneys and corner
posts for contrast. Derived ultimately from the Anglo-
Indian bungalow (see F22), the archetype is poorly
remembered and frequently mixed with Japanese and
Spanish forms. (Note the Japanese roof on No. 2970.)
Much of Kitsilano developed as the bungalow fad
reached its peak.

TATLOW COURT   **H9**
1820 Bayswater Street
Architect unknown, 1927

Clustered row houses, or garden apartments, offer a
sensible compromise between the detached house and
the apartment block, providing the access to grass and
relative seclusion of the former and the higher density of
the latter. Tatlow Court — named, like the adjacent
park, after one-time provincial finance minister R. G.
Tatlow — is such a development, with Tudor Revival
apartments grouped around a landscaped courtyard.

TOWNHOUSES   **H10**
3267-3293 Point Grey Road
Erickson/Massey, 1965

Behind a screen wall of used brick are a series of court-yards leading to five townhouses for clients of differing incomes and tastes. Each house has an individual plan, ranging from a simple two-bedroom affair to a five-bedroom house with a swimming pool. Turning their backs to the street like the Roman atrium house, they take full advantage of the scenic waterfront view to the north. The staccato skyline created by the brick posts and deep rough wooden beams is visible from the street.

HASTINGS MILL STORE   **H11**
1575 Alma Street
Architect unknown, c. 1865

This unpretentious building has the distinction of being the oldest in Vancouver. It originally served as the general store for the Hastings Mill (B27). In 1930 the abandoned building was floated to its present site on Pioneer Park and opened as a museum by the Native Daughters of B.C. The vertical board-and-batten siding is a recent but plausible restoration; early photos show the building with horizontal shiplap siding and a 'boom-town' squared false front.

D. H. COPP HOUSE   **H12**
4755 Belmont Avenue
Sharp and Thompson, Berwick, Pratt, 1951

In this beautifully sited house on a hill above Spanish
Banks, designer Ron Thom translated his respect for
Frank Lloyd Wright into something fresh, exciting, and
suitable to the West Coast. The free spatial expression
exploits the contours of the terrain. A tall and heavy
brick chimney acts as a stabilizer to which the horizontally composed wings are anchored. Thom's artistic new
plantings have matured and blend well with the earlier
growth.

E. W. SHORE HOUSE   **H13**
4791 Belmont Avenue
Architect unknown, 1937

This handsome house represents the 1930s' idea of
modernism. Architects of the Moderne Style were apparently impressed by the newly introduced International
Style of Walter Gropius, Le Corbusier, and others, and
they incorporated a series of poorly understood quotations
from their work. Features such as the corner windows
and circular bull's-eye window, and the bare geometry of
the rectangle and the cylinder, have shed their original
progressive context. The beige paint (covering what must
surely have been white) and deep window awnings alter
the original effect. Another fine example of the style —
off the tour route — is R. A. D. Berwick's house (1938)
for Isabel Crosby at 1529 West 33rd Avenue.

THE UNIVERSITY OF BRITISH COLUMBIA **H14**

a/ Science (Chemistry) Building
Sharp and Thompson, 1914-25; additions 1958-59, 1962-63

b/ Main Library
Sharp and Thompson, 1923-25, wings 1947-48, 1959-60

c/ Buchanan Building
Thompson, Berwick, and Pratt, 1956-58, 1960

d/ Ladner Carillon and Clock Tower
Thompson, Berwick, Pratt, and Partners, 1968

e/ Sedgewick Undergraduate Library
Rhone and Iredale, 1971-72

f/ Buchanan Tower
Toby, Russell, Buckwell, and Associates, 1970-72

The University of British Columbia, the province's first public institution for higher education, was created by the provincial legislature in 1908. Architects Sharp and Thompson won an international competition to design the Point Grey campus, and in 1913 they and a consulting commission issued a modified master plan urging that buildings be in the 'Modern Tudor' style to 'express and perpetuate the traditions of British scholastic life.' Construction of the Science (now Chemistry) Building was interrupted by the outbreak of war and a provincial financial crisis, and the structure remained a concrete skeleton while classes continued in temporary quarters in Fairview. The Great Trek of 1922, in which students paraded to Point Grey, cast attention upon the unfinished building. Only then were the Science Building and the central part of the Library completed. New buildings continued the Collegiate Gothic mode until about 1950, although mainly in the watered-down stuccoed wood frame version of the 'semi-permanent' buildings west of the Library. A new building programme begun in 1956 introduced the International Style to the campus. The Buchanan Building, with its precise rectilinear exterior of grey glazed brick, painted concrete, porcelain enamel panels, and glass, reflects the new tendency for univer-

sities inspired by Ludwig Mies van der Rohe's Chicago campus for the Illinois Institute of Technology. In the 1960s, Sharp and Thompson (by then renamed Thompson, Berwick, and Pratt) lost their monopoly over campus architecture. Perhaps the most exciting recent building by another firm is Rhone and Iredale's Sedgewick Library, located beneath the treed Main Mall to preserve open space and the precious view of the mountains and water. The Buchanan Tower, in contrast, brought the tall urban office building (compare D7) to the university campus.

Park your car at the north end of the Main Mall, near the Frederic Wood Theatre, and visit this and the next group of buildings on foot.

George Allen Aerial Photos Ltd.

THE UNIVERSITY OF BRITISH COLUMBIA   **H15**

a/ Woodward Biomedical Library
*Thompson, Berwick, and Pratt; McCarter, Nairne, and
Partners, associated architects, 1964; addition by
Thompson, Berwick, Pratt, and Partners, 1970*

b/ P. A. Woodward Instructional Resources Centre
Thompson, Berwick, Pratt, and Partners, 1970-72

The Woodward family (see A33) has provided the
University of B.C.'s excellent medical school with handsome and spacious quarters for its medical library, large
classes, and general offices. Most impressive is the massive
I.R.C. Three boldly stated staircase towers stand out
from the cube-ish main block. Raw poured concrete —
its formwork holes left unfilled — is set off by the yellow
metal 'piers' and the voids and quasi-voids created by
the dark glass and the grilles of the noisy ventilation
system. The building is a fine example of the Brutalist
Style. The spacious interior 'mall' contains a lounge and
provides access to five lecture halls, the library, and other
facilities.

Brutalism is diametrically opposed to the planarity and
crispness of the International Style. The transition to the
new manner can be followed in the Woodward Library.
The original building continues the grey glazed brick of
the Miesian campus architecture (H14c), but the formerly smooth wall surfaces of those buildings give way
to a bulkier treatment. The very different later addition
is uncompromisingly thrust on top, yet sensitively harmonized. Its projecting concrete walls and narrow fins
prepare the way for the I.R.C.

THE UNIVERSITY OF BRITISH COLUMBIA   **H16**
Totem Pole Park
*William Reid, Douglas Cranmer, and Mungo Martin,
sculptors, 1947-62*

This park commemorates the culture of the Northwest
Coast Indians. The Haida of the Queen Charlotte Islands
are represented by a reconstructed dwelling house, a
grave house, and totem poles. The immense Douglas fir
posts and beams and the cedar plank walls of the large
house show that much of the current method of building
in wood recalls Indian traditions. The Kwakiutl of Alert
Bay and Fort Rupert provided other poles and a carved
house frame. The contents of the park will eventually be
removed to the University's new Museum of Anthro-
pology (by Arthur Erickson, begun 1973).

MUSQUEAM PARK   **H17**
4200-Block Salish Drive
Various architects, 1966-67

The Musqueam Indian Reserve lies between here and the
Fraser River. In 1965 Block Bros. obtained 35 acres on a
99-year lease. Houses in many styles simulate gradual
growth. This block contains a brick neo-Colonial house
(by builder John Dick) ; a stone ranch-type house (by
John Blackmore, from magazine plans) ; a stone and half-
timbered Tudor model (by Roy Henkel) ; a low building
with a Japanese gable (also by Henkel) ; and a house in
cedar post-and-beam modern (by Harold Forhan). In
1972 members of the Musqueam band began the development of Salish Park nearer the river.

BARRY V. DOWNS HOUSE   H18
6275 Dunbar Street
Barry V. Downs, 1958

At the base of Vancouver's southern slope lie the flats, the level terrain that forms part of the Fraser River delta. The eastern portion, called the Southlands, is home to many of the city's equestrians. The area is zoned for 'limited agricultural' use, permitting the keeping of livestock. Just above this zoning district, Barry Downs built a low and discreet 'townhouse' with blank walls to the neighbours on both sides. The inner spaces open upon a natural entrance garden and a forest grove to the rear, with skylights allowing light to penetrate the interiors.

CELTIC SHIPYARD   H19
Foot of Blenheim Street
Various architects and dates

On a sheltered inlet of the North Arm of the Fraser River, B.C. Packers Limited provides moorage and maintenance facilities for its own fishing fleet (identified by beige masts and cabins) as well as for individually owned fishing vessels. Walk along the roadway that leads westward from Blenheim Street (just below Celtic Street) to see the many boats in the water and in dry dock. Explorer Simon Fraser passed this point in 1808 on his famous conquest of the river that bears his name, only to be turned back two miles further downstream — within sight of the river mouth — by the Musqueam Indians.

KENNETH GARDNER HOUSE **H20**
3152 West 49th Avenue
Kenneth Gardner, 1958

Brick is used to advantage in this striking home on the Southlands built by South African architect Kenneth Gardner. A crisp rectilinear block floats above the recessed ground floor. The minimalist tendencies seen in painting and sculpture of the time are here translated with finesse into architecture. The late 1950s marked a high point in International Style influence in Vancouver. Later designs move away into a freer and more expressive vein exemplified in the nearby Rogers house built into the base of the slope (3048 West 49th Avenue; by Ron Thom for Thompson, Berwick, and Pratt, 1960).

SECOND MCCLEERY FARMHOUSE **H21**
2610 South West Marine Drive
Architect unknown, 1891

Brothers Fitzgerald and Samuel McCleery, who had come to B.C. from Ireland during the Cariboo Gold Rush, settled as farmers on the North Arm of the Fraser River in 1862 (see p. 175). This cottage, Fitzgerald McCleery's second house, was originally located further up the hill. The three-bay-wide south façade, with a central decorated gable, resembles the rural Ontario house type that became common on the Western frontier. Two sets of bay windows project on the east side. South West Marine Drive follows the route of the North Arm Trail cleared from New Westminster to Point Grey in 1863 by Hugh McRoberts of Sea Island, the McCleerys' uncle.

HARRY F. REIFEL HOUSE ('RIO VISTA') **H22**
2170 South West Marine Drive
Architect unknown (perhaps a Mr. Phillips), 1930-31

Harry F. Reifel, son of pioneer brewer and distiller Henry Reifel, built the most sumptuous local example of the Spanish Colonial Revival. White walls, round arches, wrought-iron ornament, and a red tiled roof characterize the mode. The extravagantly landscaped grounds contain a bridge crossing a deep ravine and an immense conservatory with a 'Pompeiian' pool. A number of fine mansions have been built along this portion of Marine Drive on acreage overlooking the mouth of the Fraser River.

While driving to the next buildings, be careful to follow Oak Street by veering right before the Bridge.

THOMAS ADAMS DISTILLERS LTD. **H23**
WAREHOUSES
850 West Kent Street
Gardiner and Mercer, 1926-28; Mercer and Mercer, 1946-48

Four massive vine-covered warehouses built for United Distillers Limited and now a part of the House of Seagram dominate this part of industrial Marpole. Reinforced concrete walls articulated with buttresses and small barred windows give a penitentiary air. Inside, more than four million gallons of spirits mature in barrels. A close-up look at one of the overpowering buildings may be obtained by returning to Marine Drive and driving to the foot of Heather Street, past the handsome offices of Ocean Construction Supplies Limited (by McCarter, Nairne, and Partners, 1970) and the busy Marpole sawmill of Rayonier Canada (B.C.) Limited.

MCDONALD'S   **H24**
South West Marine Drive and Manitoba Street
*McDonald's Restaurants of Canada, 1968; G. Douglas
Wylie, associated architect; major alterations 1972*

The drive-in restaurant, with its quick-order hamburger
and milkshake, has become a Canadian institution.
This outlet for the Chicago-based McDonald's chain
combines the familiar sign and clean modern architecture necessary for mass roadside merchandising with the
warm brick and fashionable high double-sloped roof
(termed 'Gourmet Mansardic' by Los Angeles' chronicler
Reyner Banham) associated with domestic design and
therefore appropriate to a family restaurant. The original
'candy apple' red and white tile building, which lacked
the dining room associations, was felt to be obsolete and
consequently was renovated only a few years after its
construction.

WOSK'S WAREHOUSE STORE   **H25**
350 South East Marine Drive
McCarter and Nairne, 1956

This fine industrial building was originally built as a wire
rope factory by Wright's Canadian Ropes Limited.
Plain brick walls with a small-paned glass clerestory
under the roof are characteristic of the hard-edged
International Style — a manner that began in an industrial environment (see C28). Inside, the steel columns
and roof trusses are exposed — rather than encased in
concrete — because industrial buildings need not meet
the fireproofing requirements of other structures. The
lines have been somewhat obscured by the office wing
and galvanized iron rear extension, both added by the
original owners.

SIKH TEMPLE   **H26**
8000 Ross Street
Erickson/Massey, 1969-70

Vancouver's large Sikh population has acquired an ex-
quisite architectural gem for its central house of worship.
The design was influenced by the formal geometry of
Indian religious symbols. A simple white block inside and
out is capped by a series of stepped diagonally inter-
locked square sections crowned with an open steel dome.
Ground-floor quarters occupied by the Khalsa Diwan
Society are concealed from the road by landscaping.

Sikhs have not always been welcome in Vancouver. In
1914 the Asiatic Exclusion League and other groups
prevented the landing of the steamer *Komagata Maru*
which tested immigration laws by bringing 300-odd East
Indian passengers. The would-be immigrants spent nine
miserable summer weeks anchored in Burrard Inlet
before being forced to return to the Orient.

WESTERN PROPELLER LIMITED   **H27**
South Kent Avenue at foot of Victoria Drive
Architect and date unknown; reclad 1972

Kent Avenue follows the B.C. Hydro train tracks inter-
mittently between the Oak Street Bridge and the Burnaby city limits, servicing the industrial belt along the
Fraser River. Western Propeller Limited occupies a
group of wood frame buildings clad in shiny aluminum
in which tugboat propellers are manufactured and
repaired. More often than not the visitor will find a boat
in drydock. A sawmill once covered this site; the present
buildings were brought here from New Westminster in
1972. A walk in either direction leads to other small
factories and occasional access to the river.

2015-2075 FRASERVIEW DRIVE **H28**
Architects unknown, 1950-51

These smaller 1½-storey houses may be taken to represent typical developers' domestic work of the early fifties. The gabled roofs, squared bay windows, and small front porches reveal the persistence of traditional forms simplified by the influence of modernism. Rows of virtually identical single-family houses differ surprisingly little in basics from those of a half century earlier (compare E8). Fraserview, commanding fine views of the river, was subdivided shortly after the second world war with streets that follow the contours of the sloping land. Much of Fraserview was developed with government-financed housing for veterans.

RENTAL HOUSING PROJECT **H29**
3200 - block East 58th Avenue
David Crinion (CMHC); Downs/Archambault, associated architects, 1972-73

One hundred one- to four-bedroom units of subsidized rental housing make up this high-density project in Champlain Heights, the last acreage within Vancouver's city limits to be developed. Cluster groupings of low-rise units surround public courts with integrated children's play areas. An activity centre at the edge, differentiated by its cedar siding, invites neighbours to join the residents. All units except the 3-storey apartments have access to a private garden. The architects appreciated the psychological function of such details as porches, fences, landscaping, and roof trim ('the roof is home') and included them for privacy and a sense of place (contrast H36, B46).

CHAMPLAIN HEIGHTS   **H30**

House designs in this Champlain Heights development
offer little variation from the common scheme of a 2-
storey house with a carport or garage on the entrance
level and all of the principal living spaces located incon-
veniently on the floor above. Variations are often restricted to the choice of facing material to be combined
with stucco's basic white. The inability of builders to
provide lower cost houses without greater convenience,
variation, or architectural participation sadly reveals the
inadequacy of modern housing technology as well as the
steadfast conservatism of finance companies. As a result
countless such houses are appearing throughout Vancouver and its suburbs.

While driving through the Killarney Park district to
the next building, notice the even blander stucco houses
of the 1950s and early '60s that line 49th Avenue.

SUPER-VALU STORE   **H31**
6399 Victoria Drive
McKee and Gray, 1960

The supermarket requires a large interior space, prefer-
ably uninterrupted by columns. Super-Valu Stores developed a very efficient and quite attractive system
utilizing large glued-laminated timber arches. The surprisingly small connectors where the arches meet the
footings bear the full weight of the roof.

Typical of South Vancouver's haphazard planning,
47th Avenue (travelled on the next part of the tour) is
poorly aligned between Victoria Drive and Knight Street.

D. STEWART MURRAY HEALTH AND   **H32**
WELFARE BUILDING
6405-6445 Knight Street
Duncan McNab and Associates, 1960

International Style architecture had been considered
somewhat radical for public buildings in 1950 (C28) ; a
decade later it was the preferred mode. This district
office for the city's health and welfare services translates
the style into a human scale. The exposed steel columns
break the glass and brick infill into comfortably small
parts. It is clear from their aligned coursing that the
white and orange brick walls are not load-bearing. The
lower entrance leads to an attractive planted courtyard.

VANCOUVER CITY COLLEGE, LANGARA   **H33**
100 West 49th Avenue
Ronald B. Howard, 1969-70; Allan B. Wilson,
associated architect

The Vancouver School Board operates Vancouver City
College, a post-secondary institution similar to the province's junior colleges. This campus was built on a corner
of the C.P.R.'s Langara Golf Course — Langara was the
name the Spanish explorers gave to Vancouver. The
freely composed complex is comprised of a tall library
block and lower academic and gymnasium blocks. All
are warmly finished in textured concrete and red brick.
This design reflects the recent movement away from the
International Style (see H32) towards Brutalism.

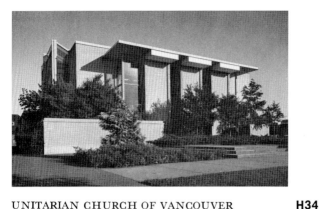

UNITARIAN CHURCH OF VANCOUVER   **H34**
949 West 49th Avenue
Wolfgang Gerson, 1964; R. Hale, associated architect

This handsome building avoids the clichés of traditional church design and thereby disassociates the Unitarian Church from the established denominations. One may contrast it with St. Matthias' Anglican Church a few blocks east at 680 West 49th Avenue (by Ross A. Lort, 1960) or the Estonian Lutheran Church of St. Peter across the street (1964), where the steep roofs, spire, and rough stonework or board-and-batten woodwork are clearly reminiscent of the Gothic Revival tradition. The *tabula rasa* of the Unitarian Church makes it equally acceptable as a home for Temple Sholom's Reformed Jewish services. Three buildings are grouped around an open court: the taller sanctuary at the north, the education building to the west, and the administration block at the south-east corner. The separation of functions and the cubic composition with overhanging flat roofs recall Frank Lloyd Wright's familiar Unity Church, built near Chicago in 1906. Unity of Vancouver (by W. D. Buttjes, 1964), located further along the route at 5840 Oak Street, likewise breaks with tradition in the soaring curve of its arched roof.

BLOEDEL CONSERVATORY   **H35**
Queen Elizabeth Park
Underwood, McKinley, Cameron, Wilson, and Smith,
1969; Thorson and Thorson, structural engineers

Lush tropical plants grow beneath the 'triodetic' dome, 140 feet in diameter, assembled from aluminum pipe triangles and 1,500 plexiglas bubbles whose dimensions were calculated by computer. The Conservatory (admission 50¢) crowns 500-foot-high Little Mountain, the highest point in the City of Vancouver. In 1949 the mountain began to be transformed into 130-acre Queen Elizabeth Park, the largest park in the city after Stanley Park. Henry Moore's bronze *Knife-Edge (Two Pieces)* adorns the adjacent plaza, whose wood decks and reflecting pools cover one of two reservoirs on the mountain. From here, the visitor has a 360-degree view of the city. The striking Quarry House restaurant (by the same architects, 1972-73) is perched nearby at the edge of the slope. Below the summit, two abandoned basalt quarries have been transformed into attractive gardens, the north slope planted as an arboretum, and extensive recreational facilities installed.

LITTLE MOUNTAIN PUBLIC HOUSING   **H36**
33rd to 37th Avenues, between Ontario and Main Streets
Thompson, Berwick, and Pratt, 1953-54

Blandness characterizes Vancouver's first low rental housing project which contains 224 units of row type housing and apartments. More recent developments of this type (see H29) have attempted to provide better facilities and design, and to integrate the residents physically and psychologically with the community-at-large.

4564-4578 JOHN STREET   H37
Architect unknown, 1914

The municipality of South Vancouver developed after 1908 into a sprawling working class suburb. This block of John Street was built up in one sweep much like parts of Kitsilano; its houses may be seen as California Bungalows without the decorative frills (compare H8). The adjacent houses to the south are similar but have had their front porches filled in. Low taxes meant few municipal services; imperfect surveys and planning caused streets to be laid out with frequent jogs and bends and uneven block spacing. John Street ended up so close to Prince Edward Street that these houses and those on the blocks to the north have their fronts facing one street and rear access to the other.

300-BLOCK EAST 28TH AVENUE   H38
Various architects and dates

The development of South Vancouver was generally less uniform than one might surmise from the previous group of houses. This block contains thirteen dwellings, a store ('Corner Store'), and a church. Apart from three that are identical (Nos. 350-366), the houses are unrelated in size or design. Point Grey's houses are normally set back at least 24 feet behind the property line, leaving deep front lawns as a kind of public space. Here in contrast the homes are often closer than 10 feet to the property line, leaving a larger back yard (frequently planted as a garden).

    The 3800- and 3700-blocks of Quebec Street, visited next, similarly have houses snug against the roadway. The small lots and tightly packed dwellings give a distinctive, almost European, character.

MONARCH FURNITURE FACTORY   **H39**
Between unit-blocks East 19th and 20th Avenues
Architect unknown, probably c. 1910

Hidden away on a back lane and completely surrounded
by residences is this 3-storey furniture factory. The usage-
restricting zoning by-law was adopted to put an end to
just this kind of intrusion; but 'non-conforming uses' in
existence before the by-law was enacted are permitted to
remain indefinitely.

The tour continues along King Edward (25th)
Avenue, whose streetscape demonstrates the transition
from South Vancouver to Point Grey. West of Ontario
Street the utilities go underground, the street widens,
and the houses retreat; a central boulevard appears at
Columbia Street; further west the boulevard trees are
more mature and the roadway curves and dips through
Shaughnessy Heights.

ALVIN E. BRYAN HOUSE   **H40**
563 West King Edward Avenue
Architect unknown, 1938

This compact house originally inhabited by streetcar
motorman Bryan represents a developer's stock design
that appeared in large numbers all across Vancouver.
The turreted entrance, arched windows, and buttressed
sides give the house mock-heroic Romanesque airs. A
Gothic version, with pointed and depressed arches was
also available (see the nearby example at 720 West King
Edward Avenue).

WILLIAM H. JAMES HOUSE   **H41**
587 West King Edward Avenue
Ross A. Lort, 1942

A cozy Cotswold cottage furnished the model for this
quaint residence. The undulating shingle roof convinc-
ingly imitates thatching; half-timbering and rubble stonework complete the fairy tale imagery. Builder Brenton T.
Lea (F23) erected three such houses to architect Lort's
designs. The most attractive is Lea's own residence at
3979 West Ninth.

ARBUTUS VILLAGE   **H42**
King Edward Avenue between Valley Drive and
Arbutus Street
Harrison/Kiss, associated archiects, begun 1972

Marathon Realty, the real estate division of the C.P.R.,
is developing this condominium housing and shopping
complex on land of theirs, part of which was formerly a
golf course. Informally grouped low units have the shed
roofs and cedar siding inspired by recent California
architecture (see I13) and now become an integral part
of the local design vocabulary. A 6-storey brick and concrete unit fills out the site. Several other multiple-housing
projects have recently been built in the area. On the
other side of King Edward Avenue stand small and plain
stucco homes typical of less expensive dwellings of the
previous decades.

ST GEORGE'S GREEK ORTHODOX CHURCH **H43**
Arbutus Street and Valley Drive
Hamilton, Doyle, and Associates, 1970-71

Delicate arches and patterned screen walls of precast
concrete enclose the domed sanctuary of this attractive
church. Many of Vancouver's 10,000 Greek residents live
in the area between here and their former church at
2305 West 7th Avenue (1930; now the Kitsilano Neighbourhood Services Centre). The community's commercial district is located along Broadway near Macdonald
Street.

TALTON PLACE **H44**
2000-block West 15th Avenue
Various architects for Prudential Builders Limited,
1910-14

Six city blocks purchased from the C.P.R. (the 1900-
and 2000-blocks of West 13th to 16th Avenues) provided
104 homesites for what was probably the first large scale
housing development in Vancouver. The development,
financed by the B.C. Permanent Loan Company (see
C30) was promoted as a middle-class alternative to
nearby Shaughnessy Heights. The name of the development was chosen by company president Thomas Talton
Langlois, who conceived the scheme after visiting a
similar project in Los Angeles. The 2-storey 'California
Bungalows' (see H8) were initially factory-built in Vancouver and reassembled on the 50-foot lots. Later houses,
including the illustrated example at 2017 West 15th
Avenue (built for F. P. Bishop, 1913), were built on the
site because the factory-constructed homes were found to
be too expensive. A number of architects were employed;
two were R. W. S. Chadney and Frank Mellish.

GRANVILLE WEST   **H45**
1778 West 12th Avenue
Eng and Wright, 1972

In recent years the South Granville and Kitsilano areas
have been undergoing a radical change similar to that of
the West End a generation ago. Entire blocks of frame
houses are being replaced by 3-storey apartment buildings and self-owned condominiums. Dawson Developments' Granville West adopts the cedar siding and
mansard-type roofs popular in private homes. The façade
is broken up by advancing and recessed balconies for
visual variety. The forty-one one- and two-bedroom
suites discourage families with children, as do most similar developments in the neighbourhood.

ALEXANDRA NEIGHBOURHOOD HOUSE   **H46**
1726 West 7th Avenue
Architect unknown, 1891-92; addition by
Dalton and Eveleigh, 1909

This large frame building is a kind of oversized single-
family house. The many pointed gables, the scalloped
shingles of the upper floor, the trefoil decoration beneath
the windows, the bay windows, and the unusual eyelid
dormer over the entrance make the building a visual
delight. The structure originally housed a hospital for
women and children. Isolated in the bush and reached
only by a path across swampy land, it was avoided by
doctors and consequently failed. Between 1894 and 1938
the building was operated as an orphanage by the
Women's Christian Temperance Union. It is now owned
by the Neighbourhood Services Association of Greater
Vancouver and serves families in the Kitsilano area.

GEORGE L. LESLIE HOUSE   **H47**
1380 Hornby Street
George L. Leslie, c. 1888

This delightful yellow house, a survivor of old Yaletown (see G2), has found a happy new life as a chic Italian restaurant. A 2-storey bay window and a turned balustrade enliven the façade. The smaller gabled house at the rear was built ten years later for plasterer Leslie's daughter when she married. Just up Hornby Street was the Yaletown Church (St. Paul's Anglican Church), built around 1889 and moved in 1898 to Jervis and Pendrell Streets in the West End (and rebuilt in 1905).

Driving Tour   I

Burrard Inlet
and the North Shore

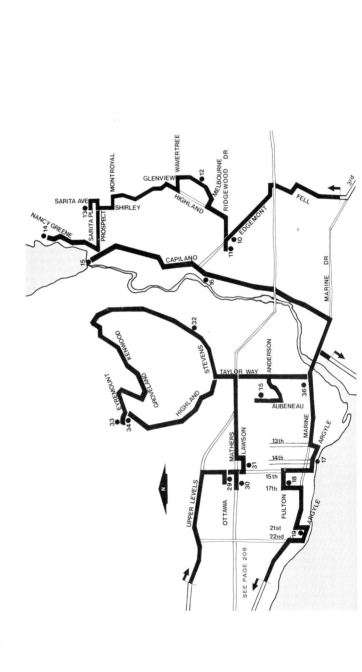

MONTROYAL

WAVERTREE

GLENVIEW

MELBOURNE

RIDGEWOOD DR

●12

HIGHLAND

SARITA AVE

SHIRLEY

●13

FELL

3rd

SARITA PL

PROSPECT

EDGEMONT

NANCY GREENE

●14

●10

15

●11

CAPILANO

MARINE DR

16

KENWOOD

●32

STEVENS

ANDERSON

TAYLOR WAY

EYREMOUNT

GROVELAND

HIGHLAND

●35

●36

33

34

AUBENEAU

MARINE

ARGYLE

13th

14th

MATHERS

LAWSON

15th

●18

17

UPPER LEVELS

OTTAWA

29

●31

17th

●30

FULTON

21st

ARGYLE

22nd

●19

N

SEE PAGE 208

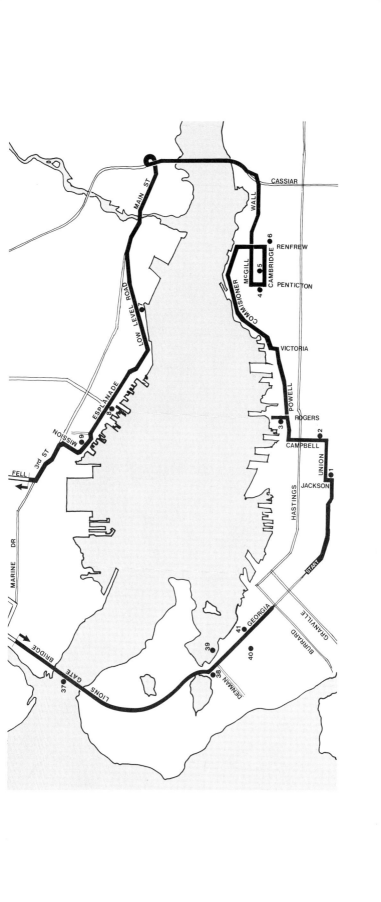

SEE PAGE 206

MARINE DR

UPPER LEVELS

MATHERS

20 CRAIG END

31st

THOMPSON

OXLEY

MARINE DR

PICADILLY

THE DALE 22
21

UPPER LEVELS

HARBOUR

EAGLE
25

24

THE BYWAY

HOWE SOUND LANE

23

TELEGRAPH
TRAIL

26

KEITH

BAY

NELSON

28

27

BLINK BONNIE

N

BURRARD INLET AND THE NORTH SHORE

British Columbia's Coastal Range provides Vancouver with its breathtaking mountain setting. Hollyburn Ridge, 3,000 feet high, extends eastward from Howe Sound, dips down at the Capilano Valley, and then rises sharply to the peaks of Grouse Mountain and Mount Seymour, both over 4,000 feet high. At the bases of these timbered slopes lies a narrow inlet some twelve miles long, the narrows at the entrance providing a superb natural harbour. Captain George Vancouver was the first European to set eyes upon the inlet; the Spanish did not notice it. After overcoming his disappointment that it did not lead to the Atlantic Ocean, Vancouver named it after Sir Harry Burrard of the Royal Navy.

The North Shore of Burrard Inlet was the first to prosper under white settlement. Attracted by the magnificent stands of Douglas fir and red cedar that lined the mountainside, T. W. Graham and George Scrimgeour of New Westminster built a sawmill in 1862 near the foot of today's Moody Avenue in North Vancouver (at I7). Their Pioneer Mills, operative in 1863, soon failed, as did its successor; but in 1865 an entrepreneur from Maine named Sewell Prescott Moody purchased the operation and quickly made it into an unqualified success. The Moodyville Sawmill, as it was to become known, soon exported outstanding timber to ports as distant as South America, Australia, and China. By the end of the 1860s, Moody held timber rights to more than 10,000 acres of North Shore land and kept two mills operating at capacity.

Moodyville attracted competition. In 1865 Captain Edward Stamp opened Hastings Mill across the inlet (B27). Gassy Jack Deighton soon arrived to open his saloon, thereby giving birth to the Granville Townsite and to Vancouver (see p. 5). In the same decade the Three Greenhorns were staking out the West End (see p. 113) and New Westminster's Royal Engineers cut Douglas Road through to Brighton Beach and the Hastings Townsite on the eastern part of the Inlet (see I6). A sail-assisted rowboat commanded by one John Thomas (or 'Navvy Jack,' after whom a local gravel has been named) linked Moodyville with the New Westminster stage at Hastings Townsite around 1866 and became the first ferry service across the inlet. Captain James Van Bramer introduced steam ferry service two years later with his *Sea Foam* (see A22).

The town of Moodyville became the most important

settlement on Burrard Inlet. It boasted the first school on the inlet (in 1870) and the first electric lighting system north of San Francisco (in 1882). It was second to Gastown only in the number of its bars; the temperance of Sue Moody kept the settlement dry until 1874. Moodyville was eclipsed by Vancouver during the 1880s, and slumped during the depressed nineties, dying when the mill ceased operation in 1901.

Much of the vast land area from Indian Arm to Howe Sound had been acquired speculatively by Vancouver real estate interests. In 1891 the landowners were instrumental in incorporating the District of North Vancouver. The depression of the 1890s almost killed the young district, as it did the Moodyville Sawmill. Considerable property was forfeited for unpaid taxes. North Vancouver repossessed much of its own land, and the Lonsdale Estate and other British interests acquired large holdings at tax sales. In 1897 the district could muster only a single resident landowner to run for civic office.

When the economy turned upwards about 1900 North Vancouver suddenly experienced a phenomenal boom. A commercial area with its own ferry service developed at the foot of Lonsdale Avenue (at I8), a half mile west of Moodyville. Around this core, the City of North Vancouver split from the district in 1906. It acquired its own commerce and industry, with at least a dozen lumber and shingle mills and several shipyards in operation by 1911.

During this time the portion of the District of North Vancouver situated west of the Capilano River experienced little activity. In the 1870s much of it was logged and the land claimed by pre-emption, but only a small number of scattered settlements developed (e.g. I21, I24, I25). Transportation was difficult. Keith Road was promised in 1892 by realtor J. C. Keith, but work was not begun for a decade, and it was never completed. Recognizing this handicap, a group led by realtor John Lawson initiated ferry service to Vancouver in 1909 (I17) and caused a real estate boom in the western part of the district. Three years later the new prosperity led to the incorporation of the Municipality of West Vancouver, encompassing the territory from the Capilano River to Howe Sound. Despite the rough topography, roads were laid out in the standard rectilinear plan, as they had been in North Vancouver. Only west of 26th Street in West Vancouver, and in the higher elevations of both districts, does the street plan conform to the terrain.

West Vancouver failed to attract industry. Determining to make the best of a bad situation, the discouraged city fathers decided in 1925 to make their municipality exclusively residential. The following year they adopted a Town Planning Act that banned industry and required building lots to be at least 50 feet wide in the eastern section and 75 in the west. These restrictions helped to attract a group of British investors who formed British Pacific Properties Limited and began to build a quality residential development high on Hollyburn Ridge in 1932 (I32). Later in the decade the same interests linked their land to Vancouver with a handsome bridge (I37). The future of West Vancouver as a prosperous dormitory suburb of Vancouver was now assured.

North Vancouver, meanwhile, fared very differently.

It suffered from the depression of 1913-14, and overspent its meagre resources during the optimistic post-war years. The cheaply constructed Second Narrows Bridge was opened in 1925, but the fourth in a series of collisions with marine traffic destroyed it in 1930. That and the financial crash of 1929 dealt North Vancouver a death blow. Insolvency followed. The district went into receivership in December 1932 and the city a month later, ironically just as work was beginning on West Vancouver's British Properties. The area found no relief until the second world war, when its shipyards (I8) became a principal military industry and revitalized the city.

The two adjacent suburbs have continued their separate ways. West Vancouver remained a quality residential municipality, with its upper-income population thinly spread along the difficult terrain. Commercial facilities have grown in recent years with the Park Royal Shopping Centre (I36) and Dundarave shopping district supplementing the earlier stores at Hollyburn. Since the 1960s a number of tall apartment buildings have appeared by the eastern and central parts of Marine Drive (e.g. I19).

North Vancouver remains home to people of various income groups. Commercial and industrial facilities mix with residences in the lower area, with additional shopping districts elsewhere; the higher recesses are residential. Marine Drive suffers from poor planning, much like Vancouver's Kingsway. The contrast with West Vancouver's overly tidy Marine Drive is illuminating.

The ruggedly forested North Shore mountainside has spawned the development of a new domestic architecture whose growth can be followed well during this tour. Unfortunately, some of the better houses turn away from the street towards the fine view. Visitors must be content with a roadside glimpse and with our photograph; they are emphatically reminded to respect the privacy of residents and not intrude upon private property.

The tour is quite long. It can be broken in the middle, after I16, and a return to Vancouver made across the Lions Gate Bridge. Restaurants are located here and there in North Vancouver, along the eastern part of Marine Drive in West Vancouver or at Horseshoe Bay (where chowder and fish and chips are a tradition); or a picnic lunch may be enjoyed in Capilano Canyon Park (entrance between I15 and I16) or West Vancouver's Lighthouse Park (after I22). The tour presents some magnificent scenery and should be reserved for a sunny day.

Distance: 60 miles
Time: 5-6 hours (excluding Grouse Mountain Skyride)

814-822 JACKSON STREET   1 1
Architect unknown, 1907

Returning to Strathcona, this time by car, we pass an
unusual group of row houses. The typical Vancouver
single family dwelling faced in clapboard and decorative
shingles forms the basis of the design. Units are com-
pressed and joined, but each retains its individuality
under its own gable. The Strathcona Property Owners
and Tenants Association that played so important a part
in the Strathcona Rehabilitation Project (see p. 34)
occupies one unit.

HOLY TRINITY RUSSIAN ORTHODOX   1 2
CHURCH
710 Campbell Avenue
Rev. Alexander Kiziun, 1940

Strathcona has always provided a temporary home for
minority ethnic groups, with only Asians remaining stable
inhabitants over the years. The arrival of large numbers
of Russian, Ukranian, and Greek immigrants in the
1930s is testified to by the erection of this building and
the change in ownership of another church nearby (B38;
see also H43). The priest of Holy Trinity, a talented
carpenter, built the pristine white structure himself. The
entrance is crowned by the onion dome symbolic of the
Eastern orthodox denominations and the crossing by a
segmental dome. The church stands next to the Raymur
Place Housing Project, subsidized housing that combines
two high-rise towers with 4-storey 'row maisonettes' (by
Duncan McNab and Associates, 1966-67).

B.C. SUGAR REFINING COMPANY LIMITED   **I 3**
WAREHOUSES
Powell and Rogers Streets
Architect unknown, c. 1902; last addition by Dominion
Construction Company Limited, 1923

Benjamin Tingley Rogers (see E18) came to Vancouver
from New York and his native Philadelphia and established Canada's first sugar refinery in 1890. Five C.P.R.
directors invested in the company and the city granted it
generous tax concessions because of its anticipated stimulus to railroad and port activity. The Rogers family
retains control of the firm today. The austere Refined
Sugar Warehouses that extend some 490 feet along the
train tracks at Powell Street remind one of the best of
nineteenth-century British industrial architecture. Rows
of arched windows rhythmically articulate the 6-storey
façade. Continue down Rogers Street to gain a glimpse
of the many other refinery buildings that were erected as
the company's production increased. Raw sugar is un-
loaded at the company dock and carried by conveyors
through the various structures until the refining process
is complete. Most impressive among the buildings —
many of which occupy landfill obtained from excavating
for the present Hotel Vancouver (D2) — are the two
Bulk Raw Sugar Storage Warehouses. No. 1 Warehouse,
an immense 360-foot-long steel A-frame structure covered
with asbestos cement panels, was designed by Swan,
Wooster, and Partners in 1958. No. 2 Warehouse, the
grey cubic solid concrete structure beside it with modernistic rounded corners, was built in 1940 by Dominion
Construction. Before them stand the modern yellow and
green company offices (by Semmens and Simpson,
1952). Just to the north is the beige garage built in 1916
by Somervell and Putnam, architects of B. T. Rogers'
grandest mansion, 'Shannon' (57th and Granville, begun
1912; conversion of the estate into a townhouse development, by Arthur Erickson and Associates, began in
1973). The foot of Rogers Street leads to Fleetham
Services' corrugated iron warehouses and dock from
which one obtains a fine view of Vancouver's busy
harbour. Shipping activity will be seen at close quarters
during the next part of the tour, which proceeds along
Commissioner Street.

PARK GROCERY   I 4
2598 Eton Street
Architect unknown, 1911

Corner grocery stores spread through Vancouver's residential neighbourhoods before the city adopted its usage-
restricting zoning by-law. Most of today's neighbourhood
groceries are operated by Chinese Canadians, who
entered this field after having monopolized local truck
gardening. This 3-storey bay-windowed clapboard building with suites above the shop (originally called Beacon
Hill Grocery) serves the East Hastings area, an extension
of the former Hastings Townsite (see I6). The district
developed rapidly with the extension of the streetcar lines
along McGill Street shortly after 1910.

FIRE HALL NO. I4   I 5
Cambridge and North Slocan Streets
Architect unknown, 1914

Shingle and clapboard siding, a balcony, and a broad
roof with wide bracketed eaves give a domestic air to
this fire hall. The tall hose tower and large doors, however, betray its function. Nearby at 110 North Slocan
Street is an unusual stucco house (built in 1913 with
later alterations) featuring a porch with bulging Tuscan
columns, a Japanese bracketed roof, and a glazed conservatory in its turret.

PACIFIC COLISEUM   **16**
Exhibition Park
W. K. Noppe, 1966-67

The building of this circular arena seating 15,000 people
successfully attracted a National Hockey League team to
Vancouver in 1970 and a World Hockey Association
team in 1973. The simple geometry and the distinctive
ring of white panels make the building a characteristic
essay in Formalism. The Coliseum forms a part of
Exhibition Park, a 167-acre site that hosts the Pacific
National Exhibition each August. The Exhibition is
descended from an annual show — chiefly agricultural
— first held in 1910. Other buildings in the park include
the 38,000-seat Empire Stadium (by Thompson, Berwick, and Pratt, 1952-54), a 5½-furlong race track, a
roller coaster, and various exhibition halls.

Just north of Exhibition Park, off Windermere Road
(passed on the tour), is New Brighton Park. This small
waterfront park occupies the site of Brighton Beach, a
fashionable watering place for people from New Westminster established in 1860 when Douglas Road was cut
from that city by the Royal Engineers. The district
around Brighton was reserved in 1861 by the Admiralty
and surveyed two years later by Col. R. C. Moody and
the Engineers. In 1869 the area was named Hastings
Townsite and seven of its forty-four lots sold. The townsite never became a going concern, and in 1911 it amalgamated with Vancouver.

To see an interesting horticultural display, visit the
Park and Tilford gardens, passed while driving to the
next building.

SASKATCHEWAN WHEAT POOL   I 7
801 Low Level Road
C. D. Howe Western Limited, engineers, 1966-68

A large grain elevator, one of many around the eastern
inlet, stands on the site of Moodyville, the sawmill community that was the first white settlement on Burrard
Inlet (see p. 209). At its prime Moodyville was a major
world exporter of timber. The mills, wharf, store, and
hotel lay along the water's edge, and the residences
occupied the ridge above, called 'Nob Hill' after San
Francisco's little mountain. The mill closed in 1901 and
burned down in 1916. Nothing remains today but the
name Moody Avenue nearby. The site has been taken
over by the grain industry, the export trade that vies with
lumber in importance to the port's economy today. The
mammoth reinforced concrete elevators of the Saskatchewan Wheat Pool (a farmer-owned co-operative that
distributes most of that province's grain) hold nearly 5.5
million bushels of grain in their cylindrical storage
vaults. The automated operation transfers 70 million
bushels of grain each year from train cars into ships
bound for countless world ports. The elevator is the
newest in Vancouver, but hardly differs externally from
a pattern evolved early in the century. The French architect Le Corbusier once praised such North American
grain elevators as 'the magnificent first-fruits of the new
age' because their engineers were 'simply guided by the
results of calculation.' Le Corbusier bestowed his praise in
1923, the year in which the Saskatchewan Wheat Pool
was born.

BURRARD DRY DOCK COMPANY LIMITED   I 8
Lonsdale Avenue and East Esplanade
Dominion Construction Company Limited and other firms; present buildings begun 1912

The leading ship repairer and one of the largest ship builders on the West Coast, Burrard Dry Dock (originally Wallace Shipyards) has occupied its North Vancouver site since 1906. Its products include the C.P.R.'s *Princess Louise* (1921), the famous R.C.M.P. schooner *St. Roch* (1928; see H3), and several of the boats operated by B.C. Ferries. During the second world war the company built more than 130 vessels and employed as many as 15,000 persons. The present buildings were erected over a fifty-year period. Most notable among the older structures are the 2-storey frame mold loft on Esplanade (first part 1914-16), containing a 350-foot-long columnless space in which templates are assembled; and the noble basilica-like machine shop (1926) of corrugated iron that is best seen from the new covered walkway at the foot of Lonsdale Street. Beyond the street is a public marina; the Seven Seas Floating Restaurant that is moored there was formerly a car ferry (built by Burrard Dry Dock) carrying passengers from there to downtown Vancouver. The ferry service was discontinued in 1958 with the triumph of the automobile. A short-lived revival a few years ago lost considerable money; a second revival is planned as an alternative to a new bridge. This Lower Lonsdale area became the commercial centre of North Vancouver with the closure of the Moodyville Sawmill (I7) in 1901. A few of the early buildings remain, such as the former post office (c. 1902) at 51 Lonsdale Avenue, a few small business blocks on West 1st Street, and the imposing Canadian Imperial Bank of Commerce (originally the Bank of Hamilton) and Aberdeen Block at 92 and 84 Lonsdale Avenue (both 1910). The area declined over the years, and is now struggling to develop its antique shops and restaurants into a North Shore version of Gastown.

ST PAUL'S CHURCH   I 9
424 West Esplanade, Mission Reserve
Architects unknown, 1884, 1909-10

This impressive Catholic church on the Mission Reserve
(one of four North Shore Indian reserves) was built by
the French Oblate Fathers. A small chapel begun in
1866 was replaced by a single-spired church in 1884.
The present twin-towered façade — formerly the official
landmark for ships entering Vancouver harbour — and
the transepts were added in 1909. Its vertical proportions
make the building a kind of Quebec parish church
(appropriate in light of its French-Canadian sponsors)
clad in characteristically British Columbian wood siding
with restrained 'Carpenter's Gothic' ornament. The
interior displays fine polychromed sculpture and stained
glass; its wooden walls have been covered with stucco.

HIGHLANDS UNITED CHURCH   I 10
3255 Edgemont Boulevard
R. William Wilding, 1958

Vertical design and the pointed arch have long been
associated with Western Christianity. In this handsome
church in the Capilano Highlands district of North
Vancouver, verticality is achieved by an A-frame roof
(pierced to allow light to flood the altar) supported by
pointed arches of laminated wood. Wood is used inside
and out, in the walls, the roof, the post-and-beam
entranceway, and the separate cross tower. The prototype
for this style of church design — also built in the Northwest — was Zion Lutheran Church in Portland, Oregon,
by Pietro Belluschi (1952).

FRED T. HOLLINGSWORTH HOUSE   I 11
1205 Ridgewood Drive
Fred T. Hollingsworth, 1948

Several post-war designers sought inspiration for a new
Vancouver architecture among compatible sources elsewhere. On this hilly site that was, in the 1940s, somewhat rural in character, Fred Hollingsworth reflected
upon the low profile and siting of houses by Frank Lloyd
Wright; the love for wood revealed in bungalows by
California's Greene brothers; and the delicately detailed
woodwork of the smaller-scaled architecture of Japan.
This creative eclecticism helped to clear the way for the
subsequent development of a new and exciting West
Coast style of wooden domestic architecture.

RONALD J. THOM HOUSE   I 12
3600 Glenview Crescent
Thompson, Berwick, and Pratt, c. 1955

In this small house overlooking Mosquito Creek, economy
and common sense dictated designer Ron Thom's somewhat radical approach to design. Plywood sheathing —
until that time generally reserved for unseen inner wall
surfaces — is allowed to stand on its own as a finished
material (see also I31). The post-and-beam structure
resting on a concrete slab owes something to Mies and
something to Japan; the clean white walls acknowledge
the International Style; the reduction to essentials without sacrificing individuality looks towards the 'Usonian'
houses of Frank Lloyd Wright. The result is a pristine
structure that fits its natural surroundings — these made
'more natural' with the landscaping in bamboo, vine
maple (which conceals the house when in leaf), and
native salal.

CURT LATHAM HOUSE   I 13
Sarita Place
Thompson, Berwick, Pratt, and Partners, 1968

The exploitation of wood and an overriding respect for
the site evidenced in the two previous houses have become the principal features of the distinctive new
domestic architecture of Vancouver. Architect Paul
Merrick revealed these concerns in this fine house. The
vertical massing, upright siding, and sloping shed roof
have been inspired by the famous Sea Ranch Condominium north of San Francisco (by Moore, Lyndon,
Turnbull, Whitaker, 1965), as have many other recent
local buildings. Here the source is adopted with fine
detailing and an exciting stacked interior space.

GROUSE MOUNTAIN CHALET   I 14
Reached from end of Nancy Greene Way
Peter Kaffka, 1965

Grouse Mountain rises some 4,000 feet above Burrard
Inlet to provide skiing right on Vancouver's doorstep.
Ski facilities, originally reached by road from Mountain
Highway, were installed in the 1920s, but the Depression
and difficulty in keeping the road open resulted in the
venture's failure. Grouse Mountain Resorts Limited
began to build new facilities in the 1950s. The two-car
aerial tramway (the 'Skyride'; round-trip fare $3.00)
designed by Voest Engineering of Austria carries 600
passengers per hour up a one-mile route to the winged
cedar chalet, appropriately named the Top of Grouse.
Numerous ski runs serviced by an array of lifts cover the
upper parts of the mountain. Brilliant lights illuminate
'The Cut' the year around to publicize the operation.

CLEVELAND DAM   **I 15**
Near Capilano Road and Prospect Avenue
J. L. Savage, engineer, 1954

The Capilano River has provided Vancouver with drink-
ing water since 1888. Cleveland Dam, designed by the
former chief engineer of the U.S. Bureau of Reclamation,
created 3½-mile-long Lake Capilano, with a capacity of
16.5 billion gallons. Walk along the top of the 300-foot-
high concrete structure and watch the water run through
the spillway. The dam is named after E. A. Cleveland,
the first Chief Commissioner of the Greater Vancouver
Water District. As a young man (in 1894) Cleveland was
part of a climbing party who named Grouse Mountain
after the blue grouse they shot on it. Below the dam,
approachable by road or by trail from Capilano Road, is
scenic Capilano Canyon Park.

CANYON MANOR   **I 16**
3400 Capilano Road
Wilfred D. Buttjes and Associates, 1968-70

Sixty rental townhouse units are arranged in crescent
form along the edge of Capilano Canyon, the deep gorge
formed by the Capilano River. Double carports stand
before the units, which are faced in fashionable old brick
and trimmed with green bevelled siding, shingle rooflets,
and Spanish Provincial carved doors. Adjacent to the
development is the Capilano Suspension Bridge (admission charged), a 450-foot-long structure that hangs 230
feet above the river. Built in 1898 of hemp by settler
George McKay to amuse his girlfriend, the bridge was
rebuilt in 1905 with steel ropes and became a commercial
enterprise.

WEST VANCOUVER MUNICIPAL TRANSPORTATION OFFICES

I 17

101 14th Street
Architect unknown, c. 1912

This attractive clapboard structure originally served as the ferry terminal of the West Vancouver Transportation Company. The firm was established in 1909 as a private venture by businessman John Lawson and his associates to promote real estate in the area. The ferry service was taken over in 1912 by the newly formed municipality of West Vancouver. The landing was moved to the present site from the foot of 17th Street about that year and the terminal building erected. The opening of the Lions Gate Bridge (I37) in 1938 seriously challenged the ferries' viability, and after a wartime reprieve the service was discontinued in 1947. Buses now use the building as their own facility. The remains of the old dock may be seen beyond the picket fence.

WEST VANCOUVER MUNICIPAL HALL

I 18

750 17th Street
Toby, Russell, and Buckwell, 1964

The District Municipality of West Vancouver, formerly a part of the District of North Vancouver, was incorporated in 1912. The original municipal hall on this site (the land was purchased for one dollar from John Lawson) was replaced by the present 3-storey building. Concrete slabs with sloping undersides project beyond the glass curtain walls. The recessed corners and the decorative precast panels on the ground floor give the building a somewhat ornate quality. The same architects built the handsome No. 1 Fire Hall (1967) behind the Municipal Hall.

CRESCENT APARTMENTS   I 19
2135 Argyle Street
Kenneth Gardner and Warnett Kennedy, 1961

This Hollyburn district of West Vancouver has been developed with tall apartment buildings. The sleek Crescent adopts a distinctive curved form and exploits the panoramic view. The southern exposure is entirely glass with balcony railings imaginatively composed of octagonal clay drain tiles.

J. C. KENNEDY HOUSE   I 20
3351 Craig End Road
Thompson, Berwick, and Pratt, 1954

The post-and-beam construction so important to progressive Vancouver architects in the 1950s is easily visible in this handsome house designed by Roy Jessiman. A series of open spaces, sometimes one and sometimes two storeys high, is developed around and through a grid of emphatic uprights and horizontals. The exterior walls are defined by an infill of glass, plywood, and tongue-and-groove cedar planks. The wall is recessed at the entrance to reveal the 5 x 6-inch posts and 5 x 16-inch beams of glued-laminated Douglas fir. Such a design was lauded in its time for its 'functionalism.' Today we can recognize that the exposed beams are in fact decorative elements, and decoration is now appreciated as it was not in the iconoclastic fifties.

ST FRANCIS-IN-THE-WOOD   **I 21**
ANGLICAN CHURCH
4797 South Piccadilly
*Harry A. Stone, 1927; rebuilt by Underwood, McKinley,
and Cameron, 1957*

A small parish church originally designed to serve week-
end and summer residents has been enlarged to accommodate the activities of a suburban community. The
small-scaled stuccoed sanctuary is now covered by architect Percy Underwood's impressive A-frame roof with
horizontal tie-beams that recall the methods of early
church builders (compare D4). The granite and cedar
parish hall to the left was built during the 1957 campaign. Piccadilly was the main street of the picturesque
subdivision planned and named after himself by English
university professor Francis Caulfeild. In 1909 he began
to sell lots on streets that were the first on the mountain-
ous North Shore to recognize the natural terrain.

THORNTON HOUSE   **I 22**
4785 South Piccadilly
Gardiner and Thornton, 1939

This house was built nearly a decade before its style
became popular locally. Inspired by the International
Style and its West Coast domestic cousin, the so-called
Bay Region Style of San Francisco, Peter Thornton
avoided all references to historical modes with his
unornamented rectilinear lines. Architects across Canada
enviously admired houses such as this, mistakenly believing that the harsher climate and more inhibited lifestyles
east of B.C. precluded the use of flat roofs, large glass
areas, and outside living spaces. Modernity need not
mean unfriendliness; the rubble stone wall creates a
warm texture appropriate to the Caulfeild subdivision.

Photo by John Fulker

GORDON SMITH HOUSE **I 23**
The Byway
Erickson/Massey, 1965

Newer houses in the Vancouver area have leaned towards one of two tendencies: rectilinear post-and-beam
structures that reflect in part the reduced architecture of
Mies and the International Style; and more irregular
compositions that are rooted in particular site conditions
like the organic houses of Frank Lloyd Wright. The
Gordon Smith house, the second residence for this painter
by Arthur Erickson, represents that rare moment when
the best of both tendencies join together. Rough cedar
and glass are the building materials; concrete is used
only for the fireplace and terraces. Four wings rise
around a central courtyard in an ascending square spiral
not unlike the superstructure of the same architects' Sikh
Temple (H26). Obscured by trees, the house is only
partially visible from the road.

NICK KOGOS TEMPLE **I 24**
Visible from Eagle Harbour
Mercer and Mercer, 1946-56

Landscaped estates have traditionally featured garden
pavilions that imitate past styles of architecture. Nick
Kogos followed this tradition by erecting a miniature
version of the Greek Parthenon on a rock bluff at the
edge of his 5½-acre grounds. The marble and concrete
temple adorns not only the owner's garden, but also the
larger landscape that is scenic Eagle Harbour. Once the
site of a salmon cannery and then a commercial marina,
the harbour now shelters a yacht club and a beach and
provides the landing for the twenty-odd families resident
on nearby Eagle Island.

ROBERT HASSELL HOUSE
5791 Telegraph Trail
Robert Hassell, 1966

Robert Hassell designed his compact home while he was
still at U.B.C.'s School of Architecture and built it himself for only $9,000. Hassell has since refused to join the
Architectural Institute because its regulations prohibit
architects from also being contractors. This house, with
its vertical siding (of cheap reject cedar) and shed roof,
has been emulated throughout the Vancouver area.
Hassell and partner Barry Griblin designed the nearby
J-C. Weill house at 5873 Marine Drive (1972-73). Both
houses overlook Fisherman's Cove, first settled around
1900 by two fishermen from Newfoundland.

D. F. PARKINS HOUSE | 26
5967 Marine Drive
Ken Charow, 1968

Ken Charow is another designer working outside the
Architectural Institute and proceeding in the same directions as Robert Hassell. This dramatic house and its
covered entranceway climb up the rocky hillside, rooted
to it by tall posts. The rough vertical sheathing, steeply
angled roof, and skinny posts recall the architecture of
early B.C. mining towns.

*Visitors are warned not to stop on the roadway in
front of the house because of its location between two
hazardous blind curves.*

JOHN CAINE HOUSE   I 27
6084 Blink Bonnie
Downs/Archambault, 1971

Precariously perched on the edge of a rocky promontory,
this sensitively composed house reflects a West Coast
desire for privacy and for expression of the site. Cedar
siding acknowledges the evergreen forest; its natural
stain relates to the colour of the foliage and rock. The
stepped contour parallels the rock massing and also indicates the internal separation of zones for different
activities. Large skylights admit generous quantities of
light that reflect off white walls and floors and dramati-
cally illuminate the varied interior spaces.

R. G. GRAY HOUSE   I 28
6555 Nelson Avenue
Roger Kemble, 1969

Suspended high above the road and overlooking beautiful Howe Sound and the Horseshoe Bay ferry terminal,
this eccentric house startles many a passerby. The bright
blue, yellow, and white plywood walls reveal architect
Kemble's conviction that 'life is exciting, interesting,
changing, challenging and colourful.' The gay colours
and simple shapes of Kemble's 'environment for enjoying
life' respond to the rugged natural setting through contrast rather than emulation (as in the previous house).
The hard geometry, lack of roof overhang, and triangular
window shades recall an earlier iconoclastic mode, the
moderne houses of the 1930s (compare H13).

    The return trip towards the Capilano River goes along
the dramatic Upper Levels Highway, built in 1956 and
widened to four lanes in 1973.

JOHN C. H. PORTER HOUSE   I 29
1560 Ottawa Avenue
John C. H. Porter, 1948-49

This creekside residence is one of Vancouver's earlier modern post-and-beam houses. Like most of the better homes on the North Shore, it is situated south of the street so that only the parking area and entrance face the roadway and the open living spaces are oriented southwards for view and privacy. Cedar, the most handsome and weather-resistant of B.C. woods, is used for structural members, exterior siding, and the low-pitched V-shaped tongue-and-groove roof. Open planning without full partitions allows rooms to flow into each other, and glass walls with sliding glass panels on the garden front break down the traditional distinction between inside and out.

R. A. D. BERWICK HOUSE   I 30
1650 Mathers Avenue
R. A. D. Berwick, 1939; alterations 1948

In his own house, Toronto-trained architect Robert Berwick made a significant departure from his many neo-Colonial (similar to H6) and *moderne* (see H13) designs of the 1930s. This house was originally more harshly rectilinear with a simple low-pitched gabled roof; horizontal window strips were inserted into the wood walls. The glazed den facing the driveway was one of several alterations necessitated by flood damage in 1948. A 'recreation room' opening onto the garden allows indoor-outdoor living. This house was admired by Berwick's future partner Ned Pratt, whose own house is seen next.

C. E. PRATT HOUSE   **I 31**
1460 Lawson Avenue
C. E. Pratt, 1948

A number of graduates from eastern architectural
schools, chief among them C. E. (Ned) Pratt from the
University of Toronto, brought the International Style
teachings to Vancouver around 1940. The Internationalists argued that they had objectivity on their side; that
their designs were, in the words of local teacher Fred
Lasserre, 'the simple spontaneous expression of a building
solution.' Thus Pratt explained that in his own house the
roof overhang (more pronounced on the garden façade)
was dictated by the need for protection against rain; the
nearly flat tar-and-gravel roof followed from the overhang (as well as from the rising cost of cedar shakes);
the wide glass area (again facing south) responded to
the summer sunshine; and the open planning of the
ground floor arose in part by the conditions imposed by
radiant heating. This mixture of explicit pragmatism
and implicit devotion to the work of Internationalists
such as Mies and Gropius led to the post-and-beam
system which local architects exploited to such advantage
in the 1950s (see I20). Pratt built such a house for himself in 1951 nearby at 430 Stevens Drive (near I32),
probably the earliest building in which the spaces between the vertical posts are filled with mass-produced
4 x 8-foot plywood panels.

M. A. ELLISSEN HOUSE   **I 32**
410 Stevens Drive
R. A. D. Berwick, 1948

The British Properties, site of this house, is a quality residential district high on the slopes of West Vancouver. Victoria-born realtor A. J. T. Taylor, at that time a resident of London, was instrumental in the conception of the development and in the formation in 1931 of British Pacific Properties Limited by British interests led by the Guinness family. More than 4,000 acres of mountain land were acquired from West Vancouver. The initial subdivision of 450 lots averaging 1.3 acres and serviced by winding streets that snake their way up the steep terrain was designed by the renowned landscape architects Olmsted Brothers of Brookline, Massachusetts (successors to Frederick Law Olmsted, Sr., who designed Montreal's Mount Royal Park and New York's Central Park). The Capilano Golf Course was created as an integral part of the development. Sales went slowly during the 1930s, even with the construction of a bridge link to Vancouver (I37). The land was consequently re-divided after the war into smaller lots and success followed. Expansion of the British Properties has been continuous. Former discriminatory restrictions have been lifted. The development retains its social appeal and has remained an alternative to Shaughnessy Heights even with the building of many cheaper houses.

The present house was one of several designed by architect Berwick for speculative builders Dawson and Hall during the post-war promotion of the Properties. This 'low set bungalow,' with a two-car garage leading to a six-room house, provides a conservative modernism that contrasts with Berwick's own more inspired home of a decade earlier (I30).

1143 EYREMOUNT DRIVE   **I 33**
Thompson, Berwick, and Pratt, 1962-63

Ron Thom designed this exciting residence high up in the British Properties. Japanese-inspired intersecting flaring roofs follow the contours of the site; their white undersides and the insubstantial glass walls (made possible by thin tubular steel columns encased in wood) cause them to hover over the land. Occasional solid elements faced in vertical siding relieve the composition. The house is unfortunately almost invisible from the roadway, but as compensation the visitor may enjoy a spectacular view of Vancouver and its suburbs, the Strait of Georgia, and northern Washington.

R. G. LEWIS HOUSE   **I 34**
1124 Eyremount Drive
R. G. Lewis, 1965

Japanese architecture has influenced local house design throughout the last sixty years. Low silhouettes (H8), fine wood detailing (I11), modular wall panels (I12), and certain roof shapes (I33) are all generally indebted to the buildings of Japan. This house, erected for himself by builder Robert Lewis, is inspired more directly by Japanese prototypes. The broad structure faced in brown wood and beige straw matting is elevated on posts and covered with a distinctively peaked shingle roof. The borrowing may produce an anomaly more akin to decoration than to architecture, but the house nevertheless possesses distinct charm.

WOLFGANG GERSON HOUSE   **I 35**
1040 Aubenau Crescent
Wolfgang Gerson, 1958

The interplay of separate masses with a varied skyline was attempted before I33 in this residence high on Sentinel Hill. Three units, each topped by a curved roof, rise up the steep hillside. Their brilliant white stucco walls make them seem to float above the brown ribbed substructure somewhat in the manner of houses by California's Richard Neutra. This house and many seen earlier in the tour were designed by architects for themselves, by-passing the often difficult task of finding a sympathetic client.

PARK ROYAL SHOPPING CENTRE   **I 36**
Marine Drive and Taylor Way
C. B. K. Van Norman and J. C. Page, 1950; principal later additions by John Graham, 1962; and by Wade, Stockdill, Armour, and Blewett, 1969

Recommended by Seattle consultant H. H. Russell to provide commercial facilities for the British Properties (I32), this mammoth shopping centre — the first in Canada — was built with Guinness money on land partly acquired from the Capilano Indian band. The original complex on the north side of Marine Drive covered 12 acres and contained about 50 shops; the shopping facilities were doubled with expansion south of Marine Drive (1962). The capacity has recently been further increased by the erection of a multi-levelled parking garage and an internal mall.

LIONS GATE BRIDGE | **37**
Monsarrat and Pratley, engineers, 1937-38; Robinson and Steinway, consulting engineers

Serious discussions proposing a bridge span across the First Narrows to link Stanley Park with West Vancouver were begun by the North Shore municipality in the mid-1920s. Guinness-led British investors agreed to finance the bridge to provide a road link from Vancouver to their British Properties (I32). After listening to public objections to a road through Stanley Park (E26) and possible restrictions to the shipping channel, the governments of Vancouver and British Columbia approved the $6 million project in December 1933. The federal government, which may have seen the crossing as a challenge to its own Second Narrows Bridge, withheld ratification until 1936. Work finally began in the following year, and the impressive suspension bridge — promoted as the largest in the British Empire — was completed in November 1938. Two steel towers 420 feet high support two 16-inch-thick stranded steel cables, from which is suspended the roadway with its clear span of 1,500 feet. The name Lions Gate celebrates the twin 5,800-foot mountain peaks called the Lions (known to Indians as the Two Sisters and to some pioneer whites as Sheba's Breasts) that rise behind the North Shore mountains. A pair of massive concrete lions designed by sculptor Charles Marega guard the southern end of the bridge.

STUART BUILDING   **I 38**
Georgia and Chilco Streets
Architect unknown, 1909

Apparently believing that this site across from the causeway to Stanley Park was too strategic to be 'wasted' by a
private house, mill owner W. W. Stuart demolished his
own home and erected this apartment house with ground
floor shops. The domed corner turret catches the eye of
every passing motorist. Below the cornice the building
becomes a wood frame version of the typical bay-
windowed apartment block of the time (compare D35).
The park causeway — originally a bridge — seals off
Lost Lagoon, the haven for waterfowl that was named
by Indian poetess E. Pauline Johnson. Its colourful
fountain was installed in 1936.

COAL HARBOUR   I 39

Foot of alley beside 1779 West Georgia Street, just east of
Denman Street

On 14 June 1859, Captain G. H. Richards and his survey
ship *Plumper* discovered coal just east of this spot; because
of its scanty commercial value Vancouver was born as a
mill town rather than a mining town. The name Coal
Harbour survives for the bay between the downtown
peninsula and Deadman's Island (named after an
Indian burial ground and now the naval training
station H.M.C.S. *Discovery*). Coal Harbour provides
moorage and repair facilities for countless boats, a landing strip for seaplanes, and is home to a yacht club and
the sightseeing boats of Harbour Ferries. Most interesting
among the marine denizens are the 'float houses,' the
immobile floating residences built in every house style
from cedar shingled A-frame to plywood split-level.

Around 1959 the city suggested that the area be
developed for hotels, recreation, and other uses. As a
result the Bayshore Inn (by Douglas Simpson and
Associates, 1960-61; Reno C. Negrin and Associates,
1969-70) was built on filled land to the east. Between
here and the entrance to Stanley Park is a site (about 23
of its 30 acres comprising fill) on which Harbour Park
Developments Limited and Four Seasons Hotels Limited
had hoped to insert a high-density hotel and residential
complex. A plebiscite held in 1971 indicated considerable
citizen opposition to the scheme; another in 1973 autho-
rized the city to purchase a part of the site.

SHERATON LANDMARK HOTEL   **I 40**
1440 Robson Street
Lort and Lort, 1972-73

Developer Ben Wosk erected this 42-storey hotel, the
tallest building in Vancouver. A revolving restaurant
crowns the structure. Many of Wosk's high-rise hotels
and apartment buildings are clad in the blue Italian
mosaic tile that was his trademark until his supply ran
out (see Blue Horizon Hotel, D34).

WESTCOAST BUILDING   **I 41**
1333 West Georgia Street
Rhone and Iredale, 1968-69

Most buildings rise from the ground up; the Westcoast
Transmission Company's prestigious head office was
built from the top down. This unique structural system
permitted the omission of the difficult-to-rent lower
storeys. The more publicized advantages are the unobstructed view at ground level, the provision of column-
free underground parking, and greater earthquake resis-
tance. Engineer Bogue Babicki adopted the proven
principles of the suspension bridge (see I37). The floors
are hung from thin steel cables (sheathed in aluminum)
draped over the top of the concrete core, thereby exploit-
ing the tensile strength of steel and the compressive
strength of concrete. The attractive glass curtain wall
reflects the Vancouver landscape in a mosaic pattern.

Driving Tour   J

Simon Fraser University

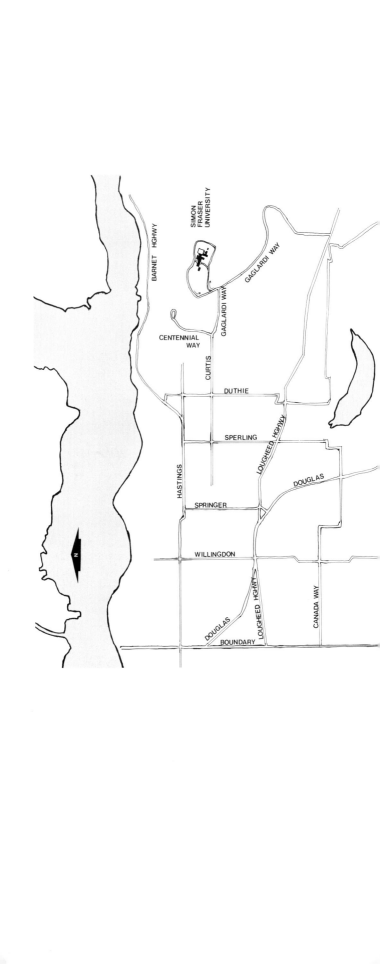

SIMON FRASER UNIVERSITY   **J1**
Burnaby Mountain
Erickson/Massey, planners and design co-ordinators;
first phase, 1963-65

The B.C. government held an architectural competition
to seek an imaginative plan for a new university. Unani-
mous winners Arthur Erickson and Geoffrey Massey
produced a radical linear scheme that responds to the
ridge-like quality of Burnaby Mountain. They determined the plan, whose continuity translates into architecture the idea of the integration of the disciplines;
they also offered a design concept for each building. A
glass-covered central mall (by Erickson/Massey), conceived as a meeting place as well as a walkway, links the
residences at the west with the large academic quad-
rangle (by Zoltan S. Kiss) and other classroom buildings
on the top of the slope at the east. The library (by
Robert F. Harrison) and theatre (by Duncan McNab
and Associates) open directly onto the mall. Concrete is
used throughout to unify the various structures. Erickson
proclaimed the influence upon himself of historical
architecture around the world; Greek palaestras, Buddhist temples, and Christian monasteries all yielded ideas
for this very modern complex. Simon Fraser, he con-
cluded, 'casts the contemporary university as an appropriate Acropolis for our time.'

In Memoriam

The following eight buildings,
originally intended to be included in the tours,
were demolished during the preparation of the book.

MOLSONS' BANK **1**
N.E. Corner Hastings and Seymour Streets
Taylor and Gordon, 1897-99

Montreal's Molson family selected a talented firm of
architects from their city to design their Vancouver
branch bank. The window pediments, arches, colonnettes, corner quoins, and the use of fine Calgary free-
stone (later covered by paint) showed the transition to
Vancouver's sophisticated Edwardian architecture. The
building was purchased in 1926 by Spencer's Department
Store, which became a part of the T. Eaton Company in
1948. Most of the rusticated stone arches on the ground
floor were replaced by display windows and a tile frieze
united the store's other buildings in the block (see In
Memoriam 6).

*Demolished 1973 to make way for the Vancouver
Square development.*

Photo by The Vancouver Province

1964 PENDRELL STREET **2**
Architect unknown, perhaps c. 1900

Time stood still for only a small part of the West End.
Here a cabin with lean-to sheds on three sides stood
beside a large vegetable garden. Overshadowed by new
apartments, the garden was protected from English Bay
breezes by four frame houses and duplexes on Beach
Avenue (Nos. 1985 to 1999, built 1905-10).

*The entire group was demolished in 1973 to make way
for an apartment building.*

Photo courtesy of Mr. Deryck Holdsworth

A. C. BRYDONE-JACK HOUSE **3**
1200 Nicola Street
Architect unknown, 1900

This frame house was built for prominent barrister Arthur C. Brydone-Jack. A broad verandah encircled the corner tower, a popular feature that links such a house to the so-called Queen Anne Style in the U.S.A.

Demolished 1973 to make way for an apartment building.

Photo courtesy of Mr. Earle Dunsmuir

K. M. BRYDONE-JACK HOUSE **4**
1220 Nicola Street
Architect unknown, 1902

Fine decoration distinguished this home of Kate M. Brydone-Jack from a common developer's house (see E8). Carved scroll brackets by the bay window, perforated bargeboard beneath the eaves, and scalloped shingles in the pediment-like gable revealed a high level of wood craftsmanship.

Demolished 1973 with the previous house.

STRAND THEATRE   **5**
600 West Georgia Street
C. Howard Crane, Elmer George Kiehler, C. E. Schley,
associated architects, 1919

This western outpost of the Allen Theatre chain was a particularly handsome early example of the Georgian Revival Style, with fine brickwork and floralized geometric ornament. The Allens of Brantford, Ontario, operated some fifty motion picture theatres. In 1920 they entered into partnership with a leading American Company; today their firm, Famous Players, is Canada's largest cinema chain.

Demolished 1974 to make way for the Vancouver Centre Development.

SPENCER'S DEPARTMENT STORE   **6**
N.W. Corner Hastings and Richards Streets
McCarter and Nairne, 1928

David Spencer erected this large building as the principal portion of his department store. By the time Spencer's successor, Eaton's, abandoned the location in 1973 to move to Pacific Centre (C1), they had spread into all eight buildings on this block and joined them together (see In Memoriam 1). The architects erected a building that they felt was the most progressive merchandising mart on the continent. Its modernistic exterior was enlivened by projecting sculpture of artificial stone.

Complete reconstruction begun 1973 for Simpson's-Sears as part of the new Vancouver Square development.

C.P.R. REGIONAL OFFICE   7
94 West Pender Street
Architect unknown, 1929

The C.P.R. encircled downtown Vancouver with its tracks. Its yards on False Creek (G1) were linked to Burrard Inlet by a spur line that crossed Hastings Street at Carrall (see A37) until a tunnel was built beneath Dunsmuir Street in 1931 (see D25). The regional office served the line's freight operations and, in recent years, it also became a major truck terminal. The red brick building followed the Neoclassical Revival Style a decade and a half after its heyday.

Demolished 1973 to make way for an expanded truck terminal.

Photo by Graham Warrington

TILDEN OFFICE   8
Burrard and Alberni Streets
Sharp and Thompson, Berwick, Pratt, 1950

The most progressive tendencies in International Style architecture reached Vancouver with a small-scaled flourish in this attractive little car rental office. Concrete foundation, steel posts, laminated wood roof, and glass walls were at once the structural elements and the finished building. Structure is decoration in this application of the 'less is more' dictum.

Demolished 1972 and the site left a parking lot.

GLOSSARY

Words or phrases set in italics are defined in a separate entry.

AGGREGATE. The granular component of *concrete* (usually sand or crushed stone).

ART DECO. A style of decoration prevalent in the 1920s and 1930s and characterized by zig-zag and geometric ornament. Its name derives from that of the Exposition des Arts Décoratifs held in Paris in 1925.

ARTIFICIAL STONE. A kind of precast *concrete*, moulded to simulate natural stone and used as a substitute for it.

BALUSTRADE. A railing composed of posts (balusters) and a handrail.

BARGEBOARD. Boards or other woodwork, usually decorated, fixed to the edges of a *gabled roof*.

BAY. A window or a door, comprising one visual division of a façade.

BEAM. A horizontal structural member. A girder is a large beam, often composed of a number of smaller members fastened together.

BEARING WALL. A wall that supports all or some of the weight of the building above it.

BEAUX-ARTS CLASSICISM. A style derived from the *classicism* taught at the École des beaux-arts in Paris; similar to the *Neoclassical Revival Style* but with more complex surface composition and decoration.

BELLCAST. See *eaves*.

BEVELLED SIDING. See *siding*.

BOARD-AND-BATTEN. See *siding*.

BOSS. A projecting ornamental form.

BRACKET. A minor horizontal supporting member that projects from a vertical surface.

BRUTALIST STYLE. A style characterized by massive composition that emphasizes the solidity of its walls; usually achieved with roughly finished poured *concrete*.

BUTTRESSES. Vertical strips of heavy masonry applied to the wall of a building to reinforce the walls structurally. Used decoratively as an element of the *Gothic Revival Style*.

BYZANTINE. Characteristic of the culture of Turkey (Byzantium) in the late classical and medieval eras.

CAMPANILE. A bell tower (Italian).

CANTILEVER. A *beam* that projects beyond a vertical support.

CAPITAL. The decorative head of an upright support.

CHATEAU STYLE. A style that revives the architecture of medieval French castles, and characterized by steep roofs with *dormer* windows and medievalizing detail.

CLAPBOARD. See *siding*.

CLASSICAL, CLASSICISM. Deriving from the architecture of ancient Rome or Greece; or deriving from any standard of excellence.

CLASSICAL ORDER. A conventional arrangement of a *column* (or other supports) and its *entablature* in which the proportions and ornamental detail are fixed by tradition. The ancient Roman and Greek architects devised a number of specific orders, the most common being the *Doric*, *Ionic*, and *Corinthian*.

CLERESTORY. A row of windows located near the top of a wall.

COLONETTE. See *post*.

COLUMN. See *post*.

COMMERCIAL STYLE. A style characterized by simple compositions with flat roofs, level skylines, and often entirely regular window patterns. The style is not consciously revivalist,
and consequently ornament is kept to a minimum.

COMPOSITION SIDING. See *siding*.

CONCRETE. A mixture of cement, *aggregate* (usually sand and
gravel), and water that hardens and attains great compressive strength. When used structurally it is usually reinforced
by being poured around steel rods or mesh to give it tensile
strength as well. Concrete may be poured into forms
(usually of wood) directly in place in a structure, or it may
be precast away from the site and then placed into position.
Concrete blocks are precast and used as building blocks.

CORBEL. A kind of *bracket* composed of a single projecting block
or of several courses of masonry.

CORINTHIAN ORDER. A *classical order* characterized by *capitals*
with leaf ornament.

CORNICE. The uppermost portion of an *entablature*; often used
in isolation as the projecting horizontal decorative element
at the top of a building.

CRENELLATIONS. Perpendicular indentations in a *parapet*.

CRESTING. A decorative band at the top of a building; often a
row of *finials*.

CURTAIN WALL. An exterior wall that is fastened to a *frame* and
has no structural function; it supports only its own weight.

DORIC ORDER. A *classical order* characterized by simple *capitals*,
usually with *fluted* shafts.

DORMER. A window projecting from a sloping roof.

DUTCH COLONIAL REVIVAL STYLE. A style that revives features
of Dutch Colonial architecture of the U.S.A., characterized
by *mansard roofs* with *dormers*.

EAVES. The projecting edges of a roof. Bellcast eaves are those
that curve outwards like the flanges of a bell.

EDWARDIAN BAROQUE STYLE. A style that revives aspects of the
Baroque architecture of the seventeenth century, characterized by a bold, sculpturesque handling of *classical*
elements.

EDWARDIAN COMMERCIAL STYLE. A style similar to the *Commercial Style* but embellished with more self-conscious ornamentation (often *neoclassical* in inspiration) particularly
around the ground floor and uppermost portion.

ENTABLATURE. The decorated horizontal member directly above
a *column* or other support; in *classical* architecture the
entablature is composed of an architrave, a *frieze*, and a
cornice.

FINIAL. Ornament at the top of a *gable*, roof, or other high
element.

FIREPROOFED STEEL. Structural steel encased in *concrete*,
asbestos, or other fireproof material to prevent it from
softening in the event of fire.

FLATIRON. A building that is triangular in plan.

FLOOR SPACE RATIO. The ratio of the total floor area of a
building to the area of its site; used in *zoning* as a means
of controlling building size.

FLUTES. Vertical grooves on the *shaft* of a *column* or other
support.

FORMALIST STYLE. See *New Formalist Style*.

FRAME. The structural skeleton of a building. As an adjective, a
timber structure.

FRIEZE. The middle portion of an *entablature,* or any horizontal
decorated band, whether or not below a *cornice*.

GABLE. The triangular portion of wall at the end of a pitched
roof.

GABLED ROOF. A roof that slopes on two sides.

GARGOYLE. A projecting sculptural ornament carved in human
or animal form.

GAZEBO. An open section of a building or an open, separate
outbuilding.

GEORGIAN REVIVAL STYLE. A style that revives the gentle *classicism* of eighteenth-century England or America.

GINGERBREAD. Any elaborate wooden ornament; often refers to
decorated *bargeboard*.

GIRDER. See *beam.*

GOTHIC REVIVAL STYLE. A style that revives the Gothic architecture of the Middle Ages. Used primarily for churches, its principal features are pointed arches and *buttresses.*

HAMMERBEAM. In a roof structure, a horizontal timber that projects from the wall as a *bracket* on which the arch timbers are supported; or a general name for this kind of roof structure.

HIPPED ROOF. A roof that slopes on four sides.

HOOD MOULDING. A moulding located at the top of a window to deflect rainwater; often horizontal.

INTERNATIONAL STYLE. A style developed in Western Europe in the twenties and characterized by a complete absence of traditional ornament and by smooth wall surfaces.

IONIC ORDER. A *classical order* characterized by *capitals* with spiral volutes at the sides.

IRON. Iron is either cast in a mould, giving it compressive strength (and hence generally used for *posts*); or wrought by being hammered and rolled, giving it greater tensile strength (and hence used for *beams* as well as decoratively).

ITALIAN RENAISSANCE REVIVAL STYLE. A style that revives features of the architecture of the Italian Renaissance period, characterized by flat-headed windows on the upper floors embellished with *pediments* or decorative frames and frequently having *pilasters* between them.

LANCET WINDOW. A tall, narrow window with a pointed arch; characteristic of the Gothic (and *Gothic Revival*) Style.

LINTEL. A small *beam* set directly above a door or window.

MACHICOLATIONS. A row of *corbels* supporting a projecting wall mid-way up a medieval defensive structure; through downward-facing openings between the corbels defenders could pour boiling oil upon attackers.

MANSARD ROOF. A roof that slopes in two planes, the lower one steeper; named after the seventeenth-century architect François Mansart.

MIESIAN. Related to the architecture of German-American Ludwig Mies van der Rohe; a variant of the *International Style* insistent upon the emphatic expression of structure through regular and perpendicular compositional elements.

MISSION STYLE. A variant of the *Spanish Colonial Revival Style.*

MODERNE STYLE. Another name for the *Modernistic Style*; also a variant of that style characterized by the elimination of surface ornament.

MODERNISTIC STYLE. A style that sought to be modern through ornament that was geometric (in the *Art Deco* manner) rather than historical.

MOULDING. A decorative element, usually a horizontal band, that projects from the surface of a wall.

MULLION. A thin upright member within a window or between adjacent windows.

NEOCLASSICAL REVIVAL STYLE. A style that revives features of the Neoclassical Style of the eighteenth century; these features, in turn, are revivals of aspects of ancient Greek and Roman architecture and involve the use of *classical orders* and ornament.

NEO-COLONIAL. Reviving a colonial style of architecture.

NEW FORMALIST STYLE. A decorative offshoot of *Miesian* architecture that sacrifices structural rationalism for delicate visual delight.

PALLADIAN. Related to the buildings of the sixteenth-century architect Andrea Palladio, or to the eighteenth-century English revival of his style.

PARAPET. A portion of wall that projects above a roof.

PEDIMENT. The triangular end of a *gable*, or a triangular ornamental element resembling it.

PIER. See *post.*

PILASTER. See *post.*

PILLAR. See *post.*

PLANAR. Descriptive of a building that is flat or with few projections.

PORTE-COCHERE. A covered entrance porch for vehicles.

PORTICO. A covered porch, often consisting of *columns* supporting a *pediment*.

POST. Any upright support. The word is most often used in a general sense (e.g. *post-and-beam* construction) or in specific reference to timber supports. Pillar is a somewhat archaic word synonymous with post. A pier is a post of square or rectangular section, usually of masonry. A column is a post of circular section; a steel member used vertically is also called a column. A colonette is a small column. A pilaster is a shallow rectangular upright support set into a wall and used mainly as decoration.

POST-AND-BEAM. A building system that emphasizes the regular use of horizontal (or slightly sloping) and vertical structural members.

QUATREFOIL. A decorative form characterized by four lobes.

RETICULATED. Patterned, often in a network manner.

RICHARDSONIAN ROMANESQUE STYLE. A style developed by the American architect H. H. Richardson in which round arches, heavy forms, and coarse textures suggest the Romanesque style of medieval European architecture without actual imitation.

ROUGHCAST. Stucco with a rough finish.

RUSTICATION. Rough-surfaced stonework.

SEGMENTAL ARCH. An arch whose profile comprises an arc smaller than a semicircle.

SHAFT. The vertical portion of a *column*, between the base and the *capital*.

SHED ROOF. A roof that slopes in one direction only.

SHIPLAP. See *siding*.

SIDING. A facing material applied to the outside of a wood-framed building to make it weatherproof. Several kinds of wood siding are common in Vancouver. Shiplap consists of horizontally laid boards with notched edges that interlock; the face of each board is parallel to the face of the wall. Clapboard (or bevelled siding) consists of bevelled boards laid horizontally and overlapping at each edge; the face of each board is oblique to the wall. Board-and-batten siding is composed of vertically applied boards whose joints are covered by narrow strips (battens). Shingles may also be used as siding. Materials other than wood are often employed. Composition siding is made of asphalt, asbestos, or synthetic materials often imitating brick or shingle. Metal siding is usually composed of aluminum or galvanized steel.

SPANDREL. The portion of wall that appears between adjacent vertical supports directly below a window.

SPANISH COLONIAL REVIVAL STYLE. A style that revives the architecture of the Spanish colonists in America, characterized by white stucco walls, round arches, and tile roofs.

STRIP WINDOWS. A horizontal row of windows with common sills and heads and separated only by narrow *mullions*.

TERRA COTTA. Fired clay (literally 'baked earth') commonly shaped in a mould and frequently glazed after firing.

TREFOIL. A decorative form characterized by three lobes.

TONGUE-AND-GROOVE. A method of connecting pieces of wood in which a tongue in one piece is inserted into a groove in the other.

TUDOR REVIVAL STYLE. A style that revives aspects of the architecture of Tudor England; characterized by steep roofs and by half-timbered walls in which a framework of wood is filled with stucco or masonry.

TUSCAN ORDER. A *classical order* characterized by *capitals* that are simpler than the *Doric,* and usually having a smooth *shaft*.

VICTORIAN ITALIANATE STYLE. A style of architecture characterized the predominance of arched windows (usually of varied profile) on the upper floor; the arches derive ultimately from Italian sources.

WINDOW HEAD. The solid member at the top of a window.

ZONING. Restrictions on building development by authorities (usually municipal governments) to control the use, site coverage, bulk, height, and other features of buildings.

SELECTED BIBLIOGRAPHY

ARCHITECTURE

Eaton, Leonard K. *The Architecture of Samuel Maclure.* Victoria: The Art Gallery of Greater Victoria, 1971.

Gowans, Alan. *Building Canada: An Architectural History of Canadian Life.* Toronto: Oxford University Press, 1966.

'100 Years of B.C. Living.' *Western Homes,* January 1958, pp. 6-43.

Palmer, Bernard C. 'Development of Domestic Architecture in British Columbia.' *Journal of the Royal Architecture Institute of Canada,* 5 (November 1928), 405-416.

Pratt, C. E. 'Contemporary Domestic Architecture in British Columbia.' *Journal of the Royal Architectural Institute of Canada,* 24 (June 1947), 179-198.

Ritchie, Thomas. *Canada Builds 1867-1967.* Toronto: University of Toronto Press, 1967.

Whiffen, Marcus. *American Architecture Since 1780: A Guide to the Styles.* Cambridge, Mass.: M.I.T. Press, 1969.

GENERAL

Akrigg, G. P. V., and H. B. Akrigg, *1001 British Columbia Place Names.* Vancouver: Discovery Press, 1969.

Davis, Charles H. *Chuck Davis' Guide to Vancouver.* Vancouver: J. J. Douglas, 1973.

Gibson, Edward M. W. 'The Impact of Social Belief on Landscape Change: A Geographical Study of Vancouver.' Unpublished Ph.D. Thesis, University of B.C., 1971.

Morley, Alan. *Vancouver: From Milltown to Metropolis.* 2d ed., Vancouver: Mitchell Press, 1969.

Nicol, Eric. *Vancouver.* Toronto: Doubleday Canada, 1970.

O'Kiely, Elizabeth, ed. *Gastown Revisited.* Vancouver: Community Arts Council, 1970.

Ormsby, Margaret A. *British Columbia: A History.* Toronto: Macmillan, 1958.

Walden, Phyliss Sarah. 'A History of West Vancouver.' Unpublished M.A. Thesis, University of B.C., 1947.

Woodward-Reynolds, Kathleen Marjorie. 'A History of the City and District of North Vancouver.' Unpublished M.A. Thesis, University of B.C., 1943.

ARCHITECT INDEX

Honeyman, John James, 122, 138, 149. *See also* Honeyman and
    Curtis
Honeyman and Curtis, 42, 48
Hooper, Thomas, 25, 56, 88, 97. *See also* Hooper and Watkins
Hooper and Watkins, 25, 80, 97
Hope, A. Campbell, 161
Horie, W. McL. *See* Baynes and Horie
Horsburgh, V. D., 41
Howard, Ronald B., 196
Howe, C. D., Western Ltd., 216

Iredale, W. Randle. *See* Rhone and Iredale

James, A. M. *See* Dirassar James Jorgenson Davis
Jessiman, Roy, 223. *See also* Thompson, Berwick, and Pratt
Jones, A. E. *See* Phillips, Barratt, Hillier, Jones, and Partners
Jones, Norman S. *See* Wilding and Jones
Jorgenson, D. C. *See* Dirassar James Jorgenson Davis
Julian, T. E., 37, 82

Kaffka, Peter, 126, 220
Kay, John R. *See* Tanner/Kay
Kemble, Roger, 227
Kennedy, Warnett, 223
Ker, Newton J. (?). *See* MacKenzie and Ker
Kiehler, Elmer George, 245
Kiss, Zoltan S., 239. *See also* Harrison/Kiss
Kiziun, Alexander, 212

Lasserre, Frederick, 229
Lea, Brenton T., 146, 201
Le Corbusier (Charles-Edouard Jeanneret), 104, 184, 216
Leslie, George L., 204
Lewis, Robert G., 231
Lightheart, T. J., 119
Loire, Gabriele, 116
Lort, Ross A., 106, 197, 201. *See also* Lort and Lort
Lort, Williams Ross. *See* Lort and Lort
Lort and Lort, 107, 236

McCarter, John Young. *See* McCarter and Nairne
McCarter and Nairne (and Partners), 8, 65, 71, 84, 90, 94, 96,
    101, 104, 179, 187, 191, 192, 245
MacDonald, Blair, 104. *See also* McCarter and Nairne
McKee, Robert R. *See* McKee and Gray
McKee and Gray, 195
MacKenzie, James C. (?). *See* MacKenzie and Ker
MacKenzie and Ker, 140
McKenzie, Robert Alexander, 40
McKinley, Kenneth W. *See* Underwood, McKinley, and
    Cameron
Maclennan, Ian, 59
McLeod, Samuel, 158
Maclure, Samuel, 122, 124, 136, 141, 143, 148, 150. *See also*
    Maclure and Fox
Maclure and Fox, 136, 141, 147, 148, 150
McNab, Duncan, and Associates, 196, 212, 239
Mallandaine, Edward, Jr., 17
Malluson, J. P., 163
Mansart, François, 144
Marchioni Construction Ltd., 195
Marega, Charles, 126, 135, 233
Marr, Bing, and Associates, 107
Martin, Mungo, 188
Massey, Geoffrey, 239. *See also* Erickson/Massey
Mathers and Haldenby, 178
Matheson, John P., 119
Matheson, Robert Michael, 116. *See also* Matheson and
    Du Gleere; Townley and Matheson
Matheson and Du Gleere, 106
Maxwell, Edward, 73
Mellish, Frank, 202
Mercer, Andrew Lamb. *See* Gardiner and Mercer; Mercer and
    Mercer
Mercer, Jack. *See* Mercer and Mercer
Mercer and Mercer, 44, 191, 225
Merrick, Paul, 220. *See also* Thompson, Berwick, and Pratt
Mies van der Rohe, Ludwig, 65, 185, 219

Monsarrett and Pratley, 233
Moore, Henry, 198
Moore, Lyndon, Turnbull, Whitaker, 220
Morgan, C. L., 56
Murray, H., 143
Murray, James A., 130
Musson, Frank W., and Associates, 93

Nairne, George. *See* McCarter and Nairne
Negrin, Reno C., and Associates, 235
Neutra, Richard, 232
Noppe, William K., 215
Norris, George, 179
Northwood and Chivers, 94

Olmsted, Frederick Law, Sr., 230
Olmsted Brothers, 230

P. & H. Builders Ltd., 164
Page, J. C., 232
Paine, Charles (and Associates), 29, 102
Palmer, Bernard C., 141
Parr, John Edmeston, 7, 19. *See also* Parr and Fee
Parr and Fee, 7, 10, 15, 19, 23, 26, 30, 67, 108, 123, 144, 162, 169
Paterson, D. R., 141
Pauw, John A., 146
Pelli, Cesar, 65
Pelman, Neil J., 158
Peters, Frederick J., 170
Phillips, Fred R. *See* Phillips, Barratt, Hillier, Jones, and Partners
Phillips, Barratt, Hillier, Jones, and Partners, 168
Plavsic, Vladmir, and Associates, 92, 160. *See also* Harrison/Plavsic/Kiss
Porter, John Cecil Haddon, 228
Pratt, Charles Edward, 79, 181, 228, 229. *See also* Sharp and Thompson, Berwick, Pratt; Thompson, Berwick, and Pratt
Pratt and Ross, 167
Preston, W. H., 43
Price, J. G., 37, 55
Priteca, B. Marcus, 170
Prudential Builders Ltd., 202
Putnam, J. L., 26. *See also* Somervell and Putnam

Radford, J. A., 38
Rapske, Robert, 166
Rattenbury, Francis Mawson, 88
Rea, Kenneth Guscotte, 68
Reid, William, 188
Reinecke, Rix, 128
Rhone, William R. *See* Rhone and Iredale
Rhone and Iredale, 157, 185, 236
Richardson, Henry Hobson, 13, 14, 15, 73
Robinson and Steinway, 233
Rudolph, Herbert, 144
Russell, Frank H. *See* Toby, Russell, and Buckwell
Russell, Babcock, and Rice, 75

Savage, J. L., 221
Savery, R. H., 88
Schley, C. E., 245
Scott, Adrian Gilbert, 45
Semmens, Harold Nelson. *See* Semmens and Simpson
Semmens and Simpson, 59, 109, 213
Sharp, George L. Thornton, 79, 100, 145. *See also* Sharp and Thompson
Sharp and Thompson, 45, 79, 99, 100, 106, 145, 178, 185
Sharp and Thompson, Berwick, Pratt, 79, 92, 115, 184, 246
Sihoe, C. K. L., 39
Simmonds, H. H. *See* Hodgson and Simmonds
Simpson, Douglas (and Associates), 235. *See also* Semmens and Simpson
Smith, Matthew F. *See* Underwood, McKinley, Cameron, Wilson, and Smith
Somervell, W. Marbury, 26, 96. *See also* Somervell and Putnam
Somervell and Putnam, 26, 66, 69, 74, 135, 213
Sorby, Thomas Charles, 63, 73, 74, 75, 77, 79, 87

Southall, G. L., 38
Stanzl, Frank, Construction Ltd., 117
Stevens, H. L., and Co., 99
Stevens, W. C., 43
Stockdill, C. Dexter. *See* Wade, Stockdill, Armour, and Blewett
Stone, Harry A., 106, 224
Swan, William G. *See* Swan, Wooster, and Partners
Swan, Wooster, and Partners, 213

Tanner, H. Terence D., 8. *See also* Tanner/Kay
Tanner/Kay, 149
Taylor, John S. D., 76
Taylor and Gordon, 243
Terriss, Kenneth G., 180
Thom, Ronald James, 184, 190, 219, 231. *See also* Thompson, Berwick, and Pratt
Thomas, Lionel A. J., 169
Thompson, Charles J., 100, 145. *See also* Sharp and Thompson; Thompson, Berwick, and Pratt
Thompson, Berwick, and Pratt (and Partners), 84, 89, 100, 115, 122, 145, 185, 186, 187, 190, 198, 215, 219, 220, 223, 231
Thornton, Peter Muschamp, 143, 181, 224. *See also* Gardiner and Thornton
Thorson and Thorson, 198
Toby, Ray L. *See* Toby, Russell, and Buckwell
Toby, Russell, and Buckwell (and Associates), 185, 222
Todd, Frederick, 133
Todd, Robert. *See* Henriquez and Todd
Townley, Fred Laughton, 167. *See also* Townley and Matheson
Townley and Matheson (and Partners), 95, 123, 137, 142, 160, 161
Townsend, Alfred. *See* Townsend and Townsend
Townsend, Joseph. *See* Townsend and Townsend
Townsend and Townsend, 50, 163
Tsutakawa, George, 93
Twizell, George Sterling, 116. *See also* Twizell and Twizell
Twizell, Robert Percival, 116. *See also* Twizell and Twizell
Twizell and Twizell, 90, 116

Underwood, Percy, 129, 224. *See also* Underwood, McKinley, and Cameron
Underwood, McKinley, and Cameron (and Associates), 129, 169, 224
Underwood, McKinley, Cameron, Wilson, and Smith, 198

Van Norman, Charles B. K. (and Associates), 91, 94, 127, 179, 181, 232
Vickers, J. E., 55
Von Svoboda, Count Alex, 88
Voysey, C. F. A., 148

Wade, John. *See* Wade, Stockdill, Armour, and Blewett
Wade, Stockdill, Armour, and Blewett, 95, 232
Waisman, Allan H. *See* Waisman Architectural Group
Waisman Architectural Group, 103
Watkins, Charles Elwood. *See* Hooper and Watkins
Watson, Henry B., 43, 105. *See also* Watson and Blackadder
Watson and Blackadder, 48
Webb, Zerafa, Menkes, 91
White, Daniel E., 140
White, W. P., 128
Whiteway, William Tuff, 16, 26, 27, 36, 46
Wickenden, Charles Osborn, 28, 73, 74, 77, 90
Wilding, R. William, 218. *See also* Wilding and Jones
Wilding and Jones, 130
Williams, H. J., 82
Williscroft, Benjamin, 119
Wilson, Allan B., 196
Wilson, Herbert. *See* Underwood, McKinley, Cameron, Wilson, and Smith
Wood, W. W. *See* Birmingham and Wood
Wooster, Hiram F. *See* Swan, Wooster, and Partners
Wright, C. W. *See* Eng and Wright
Wright, Frank Lloyd, 136, 146, 184, 197, 219, 225
Wylie, G. Douglas, 192

Burrard Dry Dock Co. Ltd., 217
Burrard Street Bridge, 178
Byrnes Block, 8

Caine, John, House, 227
Cambie Street Bridge. *See* Connaught Bridge
Campbell, Thomas J., 126
Canada Permanent Building, 76
Canadian Bank of Commerce (now Canadian Imperial Bank of
    Commerce), 41, 70, 217
Canadian Broadcasting Corporation Regional Broadcasting
    Centre, 84
Canadian National Railways, 89, 167
Canadian Northern Pacific Railway, 167
Canadian Pacific Railway, 5, 11, 19, 26, 30, 33, 34, 63, 74, 87,
    103, 133, 153, 154, 175, 176, 180, 196, 201; Regional
    Office, 246; Shops, 155; Stations, 63, 71, 73, 84
Canadian Pacific Telecommunications Building, 18
Canyon Manor, 221
Capilano Indian Band, 232
Capilano Suspension Bridge, 221
Carlton Hotel, 19
Carnegie Library, 41
Caroline Court, 116
Carry, C. C., House, 138
Carter-Cotton, Francis M., 22
Caulfeild, Francis, 224
Cecil Green Park, 150
Celtic Shipyard, 189
Cenotaph, 79
Centennial Museum, 179
Central Mortgage and Housing Corporation (CMHC), 29, 59,
    117, 194
Century House, 76
Ceperley Rounsefell Co. Building, 99
Chinese Benevolent Association Building, 39
Chinese Freemasons Building, 35
Chinese Nationalist League (Kuomintang) Building, 60
Chinese School, 57
Chinese *Times* Building, 36
Chinese United Church and Dormitory, 58
Chin Wing Chum Society Building, 40
Christ Church Cathedral, 90
City Halls, 8, 27, 41, 101, 161, 178
Cleveland Dam, 221
Coca-Cola Bottling Plant, 178
Columbia Centre, 103
Commercial Hotel, 20
Connaught (Cambie Street) Bridge, 168
Copp, D. H., House, 184
Copp, W. H., House, 165
Coroner's Court, 46
Court Houses, 47, 79, 88
Credit Foncier Franco-Canadien, 99
Crescent Apartments, 223
Crosby, Isabel, House, 184
Customs Buildings, 94, 98

Dal Grauer Substation, 115
Davis, E. P., 150; Chambers, 72
Dawson (Daon) Developments Ltd., 203
Deighton, John ('Gassy Jack'), 5, 8, 209
Denman Place, 130
Di Cimbriani, Alexander, 122
Discovery, H.M.C.S., 235
Dominion Building, 78
Dominion Hotel, 10
Dominion Trust Co., 81
D. Stewart Murray Health and Welfare Building, 196
Dumaresq, David, House, 144
Dumas, Noel, House, 140
Dunn, Thomas, 7, 29
Dunn-Miller Block, 29

East Asiatic House, 104
Eastern Building, 25
Eaton's Store, 65, 243, 245
Eburne, W. H., 175